PRAISE FOR

Hurricane Lessons

"The emergence of her new life as a gay woman is the titular 'hurricane.' ... An engaging and sometimes-painful recollection of the trials of self-acceptance."

— *Kirkus Reviews*

"*Hurricane Lessons*—much like a storm itself—is a stunning, heartbreaking, and ultimately redemptive memoir, alchemizing pain into light. This is a book of cell rearranging prose—a story many will find they've been waiting to read. The power of Willis's voice will keep readers turning the page, as the music, the poetry, and the pulse of the narrative gains steam like a storm surge and lifts off the page. Willis is an important new voice in American memoir."

—Alice Anderson, Author of *Some Bright Morning I'll Fly Away*

"This beautifully written book starts with a total loss of self, but builds toward the emboldened reclamation of sexuality, desire, and raw courage that it takes to be a woman in America today. A knockout of a memoir; a tempest of a life."

—Courtney Maum, Author of *The Year of the Horses: A Memoir*

"... *Hurricane Lessons* will blow through you like a storm, or leave you nodding because you've already had your house blown down. A beautiful, honest, sometimes messy story of betrayal and reclamation, you'll be rooting for Katrina Willis every step of the way."

—Ally Hamilton, Author of *Open Randomly* and *Yoga's Healing Power: Looking Inward for Change, Growth and Peace*

"There is no expiration on your truth, and *Hurricane Lessons* is a stunning, honest, and raw recounting of one woman's brave fight to finally honor who she truly is. If you're thinking it's too late, it isn't. This beautiful story is proof."

— Julie Barton. New York Times Bestselling Author of *Dog Medicine, How My Dog Saved Me From Myself*

"*Hurricane Lessons* is a raw, searing memoir about a midlife awakening that masterfully describes the universal push and pull of duty and desire, guilt and longing, and responsibility to others and to ourselves. With lyrical prose and deep vulnerability, Katrina Willis has written a powerful story for all of us about the costs—and ultimately the joys—that come with choosing authenticity."

— Suzette Mullen, Author of *The Only Way Through Is Out*

"Katrina isn't the hurricane in this story. The truth is. Sometimes the weather inside a life is so beautiful you don't notice the pressure of it, slowly squeezing the breath from you. *Hurricane Lessons* is a clear-eyed, compassionate memoir about coming out later in life and learning how to live inside a truth powerful enough to change everything."

— Matt Bays, Author of *How to Find and Keep a Gay Man*

"With language as tender as it is unflinching, *Hurricane Lessons* traces the quiet ache of a life lived in shadow and the luminous, hard-won joy of stepping into the light. It is a profound reckoning with truth, time, and the courage it takes to rewrite one's story after years of silence. This memoir reminds us that authenticity isn't a single moment, but a lifelong unfolding. A necessary and deeply human work."

— Rachel Macy Stafford, New York Times bestselling author, speaker, and certified special education teacher

"... Katrina's arduous, painful climb out of who she was told to be, and into the woman she was born to be is triumphant and tear-inducingly brave. No one's life should be made this difficult by a choice to love. Katrina's raw honesty in this incredible memoir was a reminder for me to keep fighting for the rights and freedoms of the LGBTQIA community like all our lives depend on it. Because they do."

— Kate Mapother, Author of the forthcoming novel *Book of Grace* and a two poetry collections, *Tell Me You Hear the Riot* and *Carved*

"We've come so far as a country and as a society that we often take for granted having queer rights and freedoms, yet that erases the very real barriers so many of us face when we come out or transition and are confronted with hostility, violence, and a lack of acceptance from our families. *Hurricane Lessons* is a potent reminder that our authenticity, no matter how valuable, must often be paid for with blood and tears."

—Robin Taylor, Founder of GenderWild Press, Co-Founder of Small Robin Press

Hurricane Lessons

A Memoir of Betrayal and Becoming

KATRINA ANNE WILLIS

Sibylline Press

Published in the United States by Sibylline Press,
an imprint of All Things Book LLC, California.

Sibylline Press is dedicated to publishing the
brilliant work of women authors ages 50 and older.
www.sibyllinepress.com

ISBN Trade: 9798897400140
eBook ISBN: 9798897400157
Library of Congress Control Number: 2025940852

Cover Design: Alicia Feltman
Book Production: Aaron Laughlin

This memoir reflects the author's current recollections of experiences over time. Most names and personal characteristics have been altered to protect privacy and anonymity, and dialogue has been recreated.

For Mom, who was always and forever my biggest fan.
And for Sam, Augustus, Mary Claire, and George,
the best decisions I ever made.

Hurricane Lessons

A Memoir of Betrayal and Becoming

KATRINA ANNE WILLIS

PART ONE:

THE CALM BEFORE THE STORM

If a hurricane is coming, you may hear an order from authorities to evacuate (leave your home). Never ignore an order to evacuate. Even sturdy, well-built houses may not hold up against a hurricane. Staying home to protect your property is not worth risking your health and safety.

(SOURCE: cdc.gov)

CHAPTER 1

Cecilia stood behind me on the Pilates reformer and pressed her legs into my back, her hands into my shoulders. The strength of her long, lean limbs drove my body into submission. Her golden hair tickled the back of my neck, and I felt a single, inexplicable spark that would ultimately set my entire existence aflame.

I was in a brightly lit Pilates studio in the small Ohio town where we'd recently relocated for my husband, Charles's job. I had paid for a private lesson from the mother of my daughter's new best friend, Chloe.

"Connect your pubic bone to your sternum. Hold it." Her voice was deep, throaty. "Even while I'm pushing you. Hold it. And breathe."

But I could not breathe. There was no oxygen left in the room. It had been consumed by her touch, her fire.

Spontaneous combustion.

Then a burst of confusion. I was a forty-five-year-old happily married mother of four. I had a big life—one that looked enviable from the outside. House in the suburbs on a lake, swimming pool in the backyard, two late-model cars in the driveway, four teenagers who lit up my world, a husband who had loved me hard since we were younger than our oldest kids. Why was I suddenly feeling this intense and undeniable yearning?

My chest heaved with the weight of this longing. It felt simultaneously familiar and forbidden, known and mysterious, natural and foreign. I searched for air as every nerve in my body shouted, *This! This is who you are. This is who you've always been.*

Out of nowhere, in an instant, Cecilia burned me to the ground, along with all the preconceived notions I had about attraction and desire.

"I can tell you're a former athlete," Cecilia said. "You have a lot of muscle memory. Your body is used to performance."

I gazed at her body, lithe, strong, and stunning, and I wondered how she could see any semblance of strength in my own. Her arms were muscled; her legs, long and lean. And her shoulders. Oh, her shoulders. My body with all its maternal excess felt so soft and weak next to hers. Small specks of dust floated in front of the wide studio window and glimmered in the afternoon sun. Dust diamonds.

"It's funny, though," she said. "You have a little issue with control. I've never had so much trouble moving someone's feet into position."

We laughed about it later, this resistance I didn't even know I possessed. When she needed to readjust me, she gave me ample warning.

"I'm going to move your feet now," she laughed. "Are you okay with that? Are you going to let me move them?"

I would let her do anything to my feet, to my body, to my life. I hadn't known it until that very moment, but I would sacrifice everything to stay in the light of her hazel eyes. It was a feeling buried long ago; an option that had never been mine to consider.

Although in hindsight I can see that I'd been attracted to them all my life—the little girls with the pretty ruffled dresses when I was still sporting terry cloth shorts, the older girls with the perfect Marcia Brady locks, the toned and muscular athletes with sweaty ponytails and bronze skin who shared high school locker rooms with me—I did not taste a woman until I was in college. I had been too fearful to explore what was in my heart, what drove certain desires inside me. I averted my eyes when my basketball teammates showered, afraid my gaze would reveal what I'd kept buried out of sight.

Eight years of Catholic school and a small, midwestern town life had been enough to lock me solidly into dating meaty football players with Adam's apples. When so many other things in my life had proven to be unsafe and unreliable, heterosexuality seemed a solid place to land. No questions, no lifted eyebrows, no disapproval, no judgment. Just an easy, expected path.

Everyone loves a pretty girl, I thought. *It's not just me whose eyes linger a little too long on a bronze-skinned beauty. I'm no different than anyone else. These feelings are universal.*

A similar thought came to me in my early forties when, teary-eyed and unable to greet the new day, I asked Charles, "How many mornings do you wake up feeling sad?" His answer—zero—was shocking to me. "You never wake up sad?" I asked incredulously.

"Never," he said.

This singularity of experiences was a revelation to me.

Not everyone battled depression.

Not everyone was attracted to the same sex.

* * *

It was a frat party at Indiana University in 1989, a drunken debacle, and she was a friend of a friend of a friend. Charles, a year younger, was still a senior in high school, many miles away, and it was a weekend he couldn't visit.

She was in my peripheral vision, moving slowly and deliberately around the room as I did keg stands and upside-down margaritas. I was so wasted, I could barely open my eyes. I thought I might die that night, but instead, I experienced—so beautifully, tragically briefly—the wild, sibilant thrum of a forbidden life.

"One … two … three …," the shirtless boys counted as they tipped back my chair and poured tequila directly down my willing throat, hoping, I'm sure, for another drunk girl to eventually escort into a waiting bedroom. I was a competitor, and I intended to win this drinking game, this test of wills and alcoholic strength. My best friends, Liza and Tyler, had disappeared, succumbing to their individual adventures.

I intended to find an adventure of my own.

After a few hours, I found myself in the bathroom instead, sitting with my back propped against a graffitied stall next to a dirty frat toilet, vomiting violently, bleached denim miniskirt hiked high around strong muscled thighs, kickass floral tapestry pumps sticking out into the next stall for admiration and praise.

"I looooooove those shoes," slurry girl after slurry girl said. The bright flowers on my feet were a kaleidoscope.

"Thank you!" I replied before I unleashed another round of tequila vomit.

And then, she was there. Not in my periphery, but touching my skin. Not in a hazy recollection, but in front of me, tangible, corporeal. Baby pink nails tickling my shaky hands, leading me out into the dark. She wiped my face, her own hands gentle on my mouth. Her fingernails shone in the moonlight, her eyes locked intensely on mine, the cerulean blue rendering me swimmy with alcohol and desire.

She took me outside on that crisp fall evening, the scent of impending autumn in the air, and pushed me up gently against the brick wall of the fraternity house.

"Have you ever kissed a girl?" she asked, her own voice raspy with alcohol. My heart raced, my knees buckled. But she didn't let me answer. Her lips met mine, her tongue on my soft palate, her hand under my shirt.

Although my heart threatened to beat through my chest, and my brain battled visions of punishing, fiery depths; I could not get enough. Her mouth, her breasts, her insistence, the lingering scent of Giorgio on her neck, the wet between her legs.

"Here. Touch here," she said, guiding my hand under her skirt. I pushed her underwear down and felt a territory both foreign and familiar. I recalled my own hands in the privacy of my own bedroom, and I knew just what to do.

"You are so soft," I said. "So warm."

I ran my finger across her lower lip, the gentle curve of her neck.

She was sweet, insistent, but not threatening. She tasted like lip gloss and freedom and sin. I wound my fingers through her hair, caressed her buttery cheek. She pushed me until I retreated, then she let me lead. I had not led before; I had only been forced, coerced. This girl—this honeysuckle savior—taught me in a single night how to take back my power, how to identify what I wanted, what I needed. How to give her the same. I might have ignored those lessons for many years, but they were there, within me, blooming, blossoming, waiting for their day, for their birth.

Although I looked for her on campus, day after day, night after night, I did not see her again. I often wondered if I would recognize her. The night had been so dark, my mind thick with tequila. Would I know her face? The curve of her neck?

I dreamt her many times.

I still do.

There are certain evenings—when the wind blows through the trees just so, when the moonlight seems otherworldly, when autumn begins its slow, steady, cinnamon announcement—that I can smell her perfume.

Although they were my favorites, I never wore those floral tapestry heels again. That garden belonged to her alone. Secret. Sacred.

I do not know her name.

I imagine it was Epiphany.

* * *

Cecilia's laugh echoed throughout the Pilates studio. "What in the hell are you doing with your feet now?" she asked.

I laughed with her, but I couldn't answer. My feet did what they wanted. My hands, too. Sometimes it seemed like they weren't even attached to my limbs.

"You're so cerebral," she said. "I need you to get out of your head and feel what's happening in your body."

But my body had proven itself to be an unsafe place too many times. I had learned long ago not to trust it. Except when I was pregnant with my children.

Growing four babies inside my belly was a spiritual experience. My firstborn, Scott, kicked me from the inside, and it took my breath away. Not because he kicked so hard, but because I could feel him. Those tiny, forming feet, those starfish hands. I rested on my back and watched my stomach undulate with the movement of him, the life of him beneath my own living skin.

I held my breath as he swam inside me, somersaulting under my ribs.

"When I say inhale, I mean it," Cecilia laughed again. "And when I say exhale, I'd like you to go ahead and do that, too." But until she spoke, I hadn't realized I was holding my breath.

I've spent so much of my life, I think, holding my breath. Waiting to exhale. Afraid for anyone to see my chest rise and fall with life, to claim my space in this world. But Cecilia was teaching me how to inhabit myself again, to find awareness in my sinew, my bone, my essence.

I let her move my feet.

CHAPTER 2

We became thick as thieves in the early days of our friendship, Cecilia and I. Many nights after my kids were in bed, I drove to her house—a little yellow cottage in the heart of Parkersville, Ohio—with a bottle of Cabernet. We'd drink that one, then one from her collection. We sat in front of the wood burning stove and talked about philosophy and marriage and kids and dogs as the fire crackled in the background. She introduced me to Wolf Alice and Arcade Fire and movies she watched again and again. We'd meet at a local gastropub for an afternoon glass of wine before we picked up our high schoolers. She was bold and loud and audacious. She turned heads everywhere she went with her long legs and her self-assurance. She bounced when she walked, her yellow mane swinging back and forth across her muscular back and shoulders.

"My God, you're so beautiful under that schoolmarmy persona you wear," she said. "Let me take you shopping for some new clothes."

She gifted me with a $300 cut and color from her long-time stylist and told me to take the afternoon off work.

"This is an experience," she said. "Not just a haircut. You need to be present."

She was bossy, insistent. She was the kind of person who believed she knew the answers to life, who wanted to impart her wisdom on others. I did everything she said. I was smitten, obsessed. My fascination with her consumed me.

On her watch, I started becoming another version of myself—a prettier, thinner, more stylish version. One who cared about eyeliner and Stuart Weitzman shoes more than she cared about being home in the evenings with her husband of twenty-two years.

When I first met Charles in high school two decades earlier, we were learning pop-swing choir choreography (complete with color-coordinated bath towels) to "Rockin' Robin." It was then that he told me about his recurrent dream.

"It happens most every night," he said. "I see this woman in a rocking chair in a dark, quiet room. Her back is to me, it's the middle of the night, and she is holding a baby. I take the baby from her and send her back to bed. I never saw the woman's face until I met you. But it's you, Katrina. You're the one."

That's how Charles convinced me we were supposed to be together. I was unsure that we were the right match—or that I was even interested in or ready for a match—but he made it seem like our future had been written in the stars. How could I argue with the stars? But also, who had dreams about kids and wives at sixteen? I couldn't even handle my own emotions. Kids were not on my radar. Spouses were not, either.

My mom often said to me and my older sister, Candace, that all she ever wanted was to be a wife and a mother. I was happy that Candace and I made half her dreams come true, but angry with my biological dad for leaving all of us to fend for ourselves, especially my beloved mom. I also found it interesting that my brilliant, beautiful, exuberant mom didn't have bigger ambitions. When I was young, I had grand plans of being career-driven. I wanted to wear stilettos and power suits and sit at the heads of tables full of high-powered men. And I wanted to be the boss of them all.

But in the winter of my seventeenth year, this mulleted sixteen-year-old had asked me to go out with him over and over again. He was a junior, I was a senior, and we ran with different crowds. I was a three-sport athlete, dedicated to perfecting my free throws and my drag bunt. He was a swimmer who played trombone in the band and nailed his dance moves much faster than I did in our pop-swing choreography sessions.

I talked at length about my conundrum with my best friend, Allison, who was on the swim team with Charles.

"He's a nice enough guy," she said. "And he looks good in a Speedo."

"But I don't know if I really like him," I admitted. "And he's already all in."

"It's okay," Allison said. "You're not marrying him. You're just dating him. It doesn't have to be forever."

"But he thinks it is," I said.

"Teenage boys will say anything to get you in bed," Allison laughed. "We all know that's true. You get to make decisions about this, too. Just have fun!"

Later that day, Charles asked me out again, hope shining behind his baby blues.

"Okay," I said reluctantly, rolling my eyes. "I'll go out with you once if you stop asking me."

I was leaving for IU in the fall, and I wasn't really interested in having a boyfriend at all. My life up until then had been school, sports, and friends, and I had no desire to change it.

But Charles was persistent, and I relented.

I always relented.

It was a lesson I had learned well the summer I turned ten.

* * *

I was the quintessential, 1970s latchkey child growing up. Because my biological dad was better at gambling and disappearing than he was at taking care of his family, my hard-working mom held three jobs to keep a roof over our heads and knock-off Zips on our feet. I would often find her asleep on the couch in the morning, medical paperwork from her third job strewn across the floor around her.

Our neighbor, Ted, was a twenty-something college drop-out who waited tables in Indianapolis while trying to figure out what to do with his life. He was both old and young in my mind—simultaneously accessible and not, in a weird vortex that swept me closely in and then pushed me back out. Sometimes he played basketball with me on the street behind our apartment building. He was short—almost as short as me—so it was easy to shoot over him. His dark hair got sweaty quickly, and it grossed me out a little bit. Especially when his sweat dripped on me. But he was nice. Sometimes he invited me over to listen to records and to have a Coke.

Sometimes Becca came, too.

Becca lived in Apartment 1-F. She was three years older than me, and everything she did was at least three times cooler. I tried to rock the Dorothy Hamill haircut, but my insistent curls and poorly-positioned cowlicks always popped out of place. Becca's short, dark hair was perfect, though, waving under gently in all the right places. When Bob Seger's "Trying to Live My Life Without You" played on the radio, Becca and I jumped on her family room coffee table and sang at the top of our lungs into her hairbrushes. She taught me how to inhale cigarettes and blow smoke rings. She told me what French kissing was. And then, with her perfect, plump lips and her warm tongue, she showed me.

And that summer—the summer of double digits and learning and French kisses and things unknown—Ted taught me how to give a blowjob.

"Would you like to kiss me?" he asked as we listened to Fleetwood Mac's "The Chain"—the consistent pulse of the drum beat pounding in my head. I hesitated. Did he want me to French kiss him? I mean, I knew how, and I liked kissing Becca, but I wasn't sure about Ted's mustache. It looked scratchy, and sometimes, it had little bits of leftover food stuck in it.

"I can teach you a special kind of kiss," he said. He was always so nice to me, and he gave me lots of Cokes for free. I thought it would be rude to say no. And it was just a kiss, after all.

But when he unzipped his pants and directed my head into his lap, I knew what he was teaching me was something much bigger and heavier than a kiss. It tasted like shame and sweat. It made my heart feel dark and damaged, unlike Becca's kiss, which made me feel light and airy, like I could float away to the clouds on a hot summer day.

"Open wider," he said, as his breathing became more ragged.

I couldn't respond. My mouth was too small, and I wasn't sure what to do. He pushed on my head, gently at first, then with more force. I gagged and my eyes watered. I squeezed them shut, not wanting to see the curl of his pubic hairs, the purple of his veins, the strange sack of translucent skin under his penis. It reminded me of the dead baby bird I'd found under the crabapple tree, its organs almost visible beneath such a fragile veil of wrinkles and fuzz.

"Don't use your teeth. Not there. Here. Yes. Yes. Up and down. You're such a good girl. You're my good girl." But I wasn't his girl, didn't want to be his girl.

I wanted to be Becca's girl.

When I was done, I nervously yanked on my cutoff denim shorts, trying to make them a little bit longer, to more fully cover my bruised legs, my knobby knees.

Later, I stood on my apartment couch and sang as loudly as I could. I reclaimed Fleetwood Mac with a soprano rendition of "Gold Dust Woman" while Candace made Kraft Macaroni & Cheese in the kitchen.

"Get off the couch, Trina!" Candace yelled from the other room. I jumped down immediately. I always did what Candace asked.

I did not want to burden my sister or my mom with unseemly things better left unsaid. So, blowjobs became my sacrifice for the family, my Penance.

My brave and beloved uncle served in Vietnam as an eighteen-year-old boy. He rarely speaks of his experience, but when he does, he says, "I always considered myself my family's sacrifice."

I understood, in a different way.

The sacrificial lamb. Quietly acquiescing for the greater good. Perhaps a bleat here or there, but nothing more. At least not for multiple decades. Voice, silenced. Spirit, squelched.

After the first kissing lesson that wasn't really a kissing lesson, Ted always gave me beer. Sometimes, he smoked pot.

When I was on my knees in front of him, gagging and sputtering and trying not to vomit the Budweiser he'd provided earlier, I silently sang the song we'd learned in church that day, the one that began, "Holy God, we praise Thy name. Lord of all, we bow before Thee ..." When I forgot the rest of the words, I switched to "Hollywood Nights." I knew Ted would not hurt me. He was my friend. I trusted him. Mom did, too.

Trust is a funny thing.

Sometimes I drank enough to throw up. I did not understand my limits. Ted would wipe my face with a warm washcloth, would tune into *Laverne & Shirley* while I rested on the couch, the room swirling and spinning around me. "Schlemiel, Schlimazel. Hasenpfeffer Incorporated." The couch was faded and worn and smelled slightly of mothballs and hamburger meat.

The next time I was on my knees and his pants were around his ankles, I thought about Paris. My cousin was there. She'd just turned thirteen and in her family, when you became a teenager, you got to travel where you most wanted to go. I would have picked Paris, too. After seeing the much less impressive replica at King's Island every summer, I had a burning desire to see the real Eiffel Tower. I'd get myself there someday. I was certain of it. Blowjobs were just part of the dues I had to pay before my eventual departure.

"You're a good girl, Katrina," Ted said to me after, breath coming in ragged bursts, smoothing my hair as I rested on his couch. My head was swimmy, and my stomach rolled. I did not like beer, but I was grateful for the buzz. I carried that knowledge throughout my life—the blessing of the booze, the inhibition, the forgetting, the sleep, the black hole of nothingness.

"Thank you," I said, and I meant it. I wanted to be a good girl.

And I could do anything when I was drunk.

Anything.

"I know you won't tell. You promised me you wouldn't. I trust you."

"I won't tell," I said.

He was right to trust me. I would not tell. I didn't even know which words to use. I learned that my body could do anything, even when it was made to do things best left unsaid. My mind saved me from the reality, the Confessional saved me from hell.

The conscious decision to spit or swallow came after I'd learned how to control the physical reaction of my body, my gag reflex.

Ingest? Expel?

Blowjobs as a metaphor for life.

During those days, my mom had a recurrent dream. She spoke of it often until I could see it all play out in Technicolor in my own mind, waking me again and again.

"We all have bad dreams, Sweetie. Go back to bed."

"Can't I just sleep with you?" I asked. "Just tonight?"

In Mom's dream—the one that became my own—she fell through a thin layer of ice and was unable to find the hole that would provide oxygen and escape, the one her own body had made. Her graceful hands pounded at the frozen blue in slow motion, painted fingernails blood red beneath the murky waters, her mouth in the shape of an "O," calling silently, frantically for help. Candace and I looked at her from above, paralyzed in the cold, unable to fathom how to save our beloved, our tether to this precious, precarious earth. Sometimes, we didn't even see her as we glided by, holding hands, the blades on our skates, sharp and thin.

Life can be that way. The ones we love, struggling for breath, for a stronghold. And we, staring blindly at the battle happening beneath our feet, not understanding, not comprehending, until it is too late.

In the big scheme of things, blowjobs aren't so bad. They are not world hunger. They are not crushing poverty. They are not war. They are not natural disasters arriving unexpectedly in the night to steal those we love most. They are not genocide or debilitating disease or death.

But they are a private shame, a black mark on a soul that strived for Clorox white. They are a chip in a Rosary bead, the corner that catches the tip of your finger as it traces its prayerful path. They are a knowledge beyond accumulated years, a dicey book snuck from the bowels of the library's adult section, a queasiness at the base of your belly that causes your hands to sweat and your head to swirl.

They are a rock violently thrown in raging winds that leaves a crack on the windshield of a young life.

Of my young life.

* * *

On our first date in 1987, Charles drove me from Grayfield to Olive Garden on the East side of Indianapolis with his brand-new driver's license in his wallet, and we saw *Moonstruck* after. We had planned to see *Good Morning, Vietnam*, but when we discovered it was sold out, Charles thought the rom-com starring Cher and Nicholas Cage was a romantic sign from the heavens. We shared a large popcorn even though I would have preferred having my own. When he held my hand in the theater, I was a little unnerved and more than unsure. On our second date, he made a three-course meal for me. He had already learned the way to my heart was through my stomach.

Later in the school year, we were cast opposite each other in our spring production of *Fiddler on the Roof*. He was the Perchik to my Hodel, and we sang "Now I Have Everything" while our director taught us how to gaze lovingly and believingly into each other's eyes. We joked backstage and shared his mom's seasoned oyster crackers in between acts.

When he sang the line about wanting a wife, he squeezed my hands tightly and closed his eyes. When I sang the following line about assuring him I'd been there all along, I looked away and made sure I hit my high note perfectly. Our goals and dreams had always been a little misaligned, but more than two decades later, we were still together.

In our earliest days, he needed someone to care for, and I needed a caretaker. I had been craving the love and presence of a father my entire life, and he filled that need with his attentiveness and adoration. We slipped easily into our codependency, wearing it like a protective cloak. Did we love each other? Of course. In the only ways we knew how as young teenagers. Did we leave room for growth, for new roles, for shifts in responsibility? Not much. We accepted our roles, memorized all our lines, and mistakenly believed our show would run forever, no need for an understudy, no final curtain calls.

We sang to each other—voices clear and strong and steady—about everything being *right at hand, simple and clear.* Sweat trickled down my cheek under the hot, bright lights and created a tear track in my stage makeup. We were seventeen and sixteen, just babies. We thought we knew so much. We knew so very little.

* * *

As I grew closer to Cecilia, Charles, understandably, became frustrated with all the time I spent away from home.

"You're never here, Katrina," he said. "I miss you."

I thought about all the nights and weekends he had been gone as he pursued his Master's degree, then his EdD. I thought about the endless days of taking care of four children under the age of five, of breakfasts followed by play time followed by lunch followed by naps that were never aligned followed by afternoons of errands and buckling four kids into four car seats again and again and again followed by dinner and dishes and bath time and bedtime and falling into my own bed, exhausted and spent, only to do it all again the next day and the next and the next.

I would shove a crying baby into Charles's arms the second he'd walk through the door at 9:00 PM after chaperoning a basketball game or arriving home from a weekend with cohorts at IU. My time was not my own. My body was not my own. I begged for a moment of peace, of solitude. He told me once that he resented me not welcoming him home with open arms. That he needed me, too. But I also needed me. And there was no me left to give.

The old adage that the days are long but the years are short had never been felt more deeply than when I supported Charles at home as he pursued his educational and career goals.

"The kids are so young, they'll never remember how much I'm gone," he said.

"But I'll remember," I replied, shocked that he didn't seem to consider that irrefutable fact.

And I did. In this moment when our teenagers were self-sufficient and I was enjoying a new friendship, I remembered all those tedious, lonely moments when it was just me and four beautiful, needy little creatures who required every ounce of my attention. I remembered uprooting my family and moving to Mississippi when Charles decided he needed a career change. I remembered moving everyone back to the Midwest. I remembered how badly I wanted to pursue my MFA, but there was never time, and there was never any extra money. I remembered the jobs and the career growth I had sacrificed for the good of my family, for the sake of survival.

I remembered.

"Charles, you've had so much. You've had big careers and big diplomas and work travel and so many evenings of chaperoning all to yourself. I just want a friend."

"Is she just a friend?" he asked.

"Of course!" I said. "I haven't had a friend in so long. You know how much I've missed Susan. Please don't pressure me into giving Cecilia up, too."

Susan was my closest friend when our children were young. We spent our days together while our seven kids played and squealed and cried and asked for Band-Aids and Welch's Fruit Snacks.

We laughed time and time again about the day, Austin—never one to ask for things outright—toddled up to Susan and said, "Whew. It's really hot today."

"It sure is," Susan agreed, wiping auburn curls from his sweaty brow.

"Remember when it was really hot the other day and we had those popsicles?"

"I sure do," Susan said.

"Those popsicles really tasted good," Austin said.

And of course, Susan opened the freezer and took out a popsicle for my sweet boy.

We'd parted ways—painfully—before our family of six moved to Mississippi when Charles landed a new, faraway job as a college professor. But Charles never really noticed all the time Susan and I had spent together because he was busy building his own life, his own career. Now that his chosen path of higher education required less of his time, he wanted more of me. And now that the kids were older and more self-sufficient, I wanted more, too. More time for myself. More time to explore. More time to figure out what I really wanted my life to look like from this point forward. We were far from aligned.

"I know you need people more than I do," he said. "You always have. But you've always been the only one I need."

I choked back some of the words I wanted to say. Words about how I'd been the only person who had enabled all his educational and career dreams to come to fruition. Words about how he never would have been able to achieve what he did if I hadn't been managing and tending to the house and the kids for so many years. Words about how it wasn't really fair to continue to rely on me as the one and only person he needed. Words about how stifling that felt at a time when I was ready to spread my wings a little, to take my turn at life.

"That's hard," I said instead. "It's a lot. That's a big load for me to carry. There are a lot of expectations in that statement."

"So my love and devotion to you are burdensome?" he asked. "Wow."

I sighed. "I never said that." I'd already grown weary of the conversation and the guilt-ridden turn it had taken. My patience with Charles had grown thin over the past year as we adjusted to him being home more often than not in his new professional role. "I just said it's a lot to ask of one person. What about you? Why don't you find a friend and go grab a beer? Wouldn't that be nice?"

"What I want is my wife," he said. "And I want her to want me."

"Charles, please," I said. "That's really unfair. It's not that I don't want you. It's that I want other things and other people in my life as well."

"Are you in love with her?" he asked. "Do you want her to be your girlfriend?"

I stumbled over my reply. *Did I? Did I want a girlfriend? Did I want that girlfriend to be Cecilia? Did he understand my desires better than I did?*

"Why are you asking that? She's my friend."

"I'm asking that because I can be many things for you. I can be your lover and your husband and your friend. But if you want a girlfriend, I can't be that."

"I don't expect you to be," I said. "I never said I wanted to have a girlfriend. That came from you."

"Seriously, Katrina," he said. "If you want a girlfriend, go have a girlfriend. I just don't want you to forget about me."

"What are you saying?" I asked.

"I'm saying don't leave me behind. Just remember that I'm your number one, like you'll always be my number one. You've been attracted to women since I've known you—we both know that. Just keep me first. And if you want me to ... you know, take part in that relationship, I would like that." A smirk. Then a wink.

There it was. The Charles who had always said being with two women was every man's fantasy, including his own. He might have given me permission to pursue a desire that had possibly been buried deep within me, but the caveat was that he got to be a part of it, too.

"Whatever, Charles," I said. "That's not my plan."

And at that moment in time, I was telling him the truth.

* * *

"I don't know if we're meant to love just one person in this lifetime," Cecilia said later that week as we shared glasses of wine, too expensive for me to buy. She spoke of her Russian lover, his smooth chest, his lollipop cock, their volatile fights. I was simultaneously intrigued by and scared of her. She was reckless, impulsive, independent, dangerous. She was passionate—both in her love and in her anger. She frightened and excited me at the same time. And when she spoke knowingly about the lie of monogamy, I knew she was right.

Because for more than twenty years, I had loved my husband. And for a lifetime, unbeknownst to me until that moment, I had loved her, too.

Had Charles unleashed this with his permission? Had he opened up a Pandora's Box in me that I could no longer ignore? Had it always been there inside me, locked and unattainable until he gave me the key?

It was a deeper knowing, this passion for her. It was in my bones, my tissue, my sinew.

I could not imagine a life without him.

I could not live without her.

When he fucked me slow and sweet in those days, it was her face I saw. When his hands were on me, in me, it was her graceful fingers I imagined. There was so much betrayal in my bed. I was with him intimately, but all I could think about was her.

Cecilia and I watched a movie together that first night of my knowing. Side by side on her bed, propped with mounds of cloud-like pillows, glasses of red in our hands, as the characters played their pre-scripted parts. But I could not concentrate because my face was on fire. I rested my head on her shoulder, my unruly curls mixing with her straight spun gold, and I dared not breathe. I was afraid to remind her I was there. I was afraid she'd ask me to leave. And I never, ever wanted to leave.

We fell asleep there together as the movie played on, touching, but not touching. Knowing, but not acting.

I was a storm inside, swirling, thundering, positioned to destroy everything in my path. I swallowed the rain and wind in the gut of me, careful not to leave irreparable devastation in my wake, knowing it was destined to happen anyway.

When I woke at 2:00 AM to head home to the life I had worked so hard to create, I didn't want to leave her.

My legs, heavy with hesitation, could barely hold the quivering, drowning body of me.

I tucked her in, kissed her cheek, rested my hand on her perfect shoulder, traced the lines of her well-defined muscles. It burned my fingers, her flesh. Her skin marked mine; a branding, a tattoo.

I drove home unsteadily even though the wine had long since been absorbed into my bloodstream. Vance Joy sang of elegance and electricity.

And I wept, breath ragged and reluctant, bursting out in waves. I wiped the tears away with my hands, the ones that had so recently touched her skin. They crackled and singed as fire met water.

I was still burning up in her flames.

CHAPTER 3

Cecilia's newly acquired pied-à-terre in SoHo was like nothing I'd ever seen, and I was thrilled to be able to visit for a long weekend. It was a luxurious space right out of a movie set where the elevator opened directly into her gorgeous, spacious fourth floor apartment with high ceilings, tall windows, and an ultra-modern kitchen. Beck played on the sound system, the white countertops gleamed, and the city bustled beneath us.

On her dining room table sat the wooden wine holder I'd bought and shipped for a housewarming gift. It was beautifully crafted and had cost much more than I should have spent, but I didn't want to give her anything cheap, anything undesirable.

"Jonah Hill lived here before me," she said. "He really trashed the place, so we have a lot of work to do."

I never knew whether to believe Cecilia or not. Her stories were often exaggerated and overblown. She talked a great deal about her encounters with celebrities, and I could never discern what was real and what was not. When I first met her, she told me she'd trained Hilary Swank for her role in *Million Dollar Baby*. I'd believed her because I wanted it to be true. She was magic to me, and her fanciful stories kept that magic alive.

So far, 2016 had been a year of dreams, and Cecilia was a huge part of that landscape. My debut novel, *Parting Gifts*, had been published in the spring. It was a book I'd worked on for years, inspired by the true, tragic story of a former colleague and friend. My dream of being an author—which I'd begun working toward at age eight with my original "autobiography"—had finally come to fruition.

My publicist had arranged a multi-city tour over the summer, and I was thrilled with the prospect of flying from city to city, meeting new readers, sharing pieces of myself and my story. One stop was scheduled for San Francisco—a place Cecilia and I had often talked of visiting together.

Charles and the kids accompanied me where they could during my tour—Indianapolis, Chicago—but the longer trips were just not financially feasible for six of us. So one night while discussing the San Francisco stop over wine at her place, Cecilia had agreed to fly there with me.

"We're going to have a blast!" she said. "I can't wait to hang out in San Francisco with my famous author friend."

"I'm so excited, too!" I said. "I can't believe you've never been to San Francisco. You're going to love it!"

But when it came time to book her airline ticket, Cecilia, in a fashion that had of late become very familiar, backed out. She had recently canceled our plans to attend an Indigo Girls concert together, leaving me stuck with unused tickets. She was also in the habit of inviting me in the morning to hang out in the evening, only to cancel later because she was too tired, too stressed, too something.

"It's just really bad timing," she said. "I'm moving into my new apartment in New York, and I need to be there to greet the movers."

I knew she was purchasing that apartment with her ex-husband, the deep pockets that supported her larger-than-life existence. Their relationship was so foreign to me. Jed said he didn't care who she slept with as long as her boyfriend wasn't passed out drunk on his front lawn in the morning. Cecilia willingly accepted the expensive gifts he bestowed on her: vacation homes, luxury cars, designer clothes, and jewelry.

"Can't Jed meet the movers?" I asked.

"This is important to me, Katrina," she said. "I can't go to California."

I was disappointed with her cancellation, with her choosing her furniture over my book tour, but I still desperately wanted to see her. So, at her request, I booked a ticket from San Francisco to New York after my reading and before my scheduled trip to Portland. A cross-country flight times two just to see her. I would have done anything to be with her, to breathe her air.

"You're flying from California to New York? For two days? Then back to the West Coast? That's ridiculous, Katrina," Charles said. "Not only are you wasting your time, but you're wasting our money."

"Maybe I am," I said. "But I'm doing it. It's my money, too, and I work as hard as you do. And I don't get my summers off." I was always trying to justify myself to him—to justify my spending, my dreams, my desires, my frustrations.

"What is it about her?" he asked.

"I can't articulate it," I said. "She's like no one I've ever known."

"Are you two having sex?" Charles's mind often went directly to sex. It had ever since I'd known him.

"No!" I said adamantly. "We're just friends. I enjoy her company. And yes, I'm attracted to her, but she's straight. We're friends."

"You know why you're attracted to her, don't you?" he asked with a mean edge to his voice. "Because she makes you feel like you're not the poor, little white trash Weston Village girl that you'll always be. Your rich cousins won't wine and dine you in New York, but she will. That's all you've ever really wanted, isn't it? To be more than you really are? To pretend that you have that kind of money so that everyone will love you?"

"Why would you say that to me?" I asked. "Why would you be so cruel?"

"Because it's true. Because she's taking you away from me, and you're allowing it to happen. Because I've spent my whole life loving and supporting you and trying to make you feel beautiful and wanted. And none of that matters because nothing is ever enough for you. You just take, take, take to fill some insatiable hole that your dad left in you."

His words, the most painful of all. He knew me well enough to know where all my deepest wounds were. And because I chose to spend my time with Cecilia—who he was learning to resent and despise—he was no longer afraid to open them up and let them bleed.

* * *

Charles knew all the details about my childhood and how my single mother willingly showered us with everything she was capable of providing—laughter, encouragement, food, a roof over our heads, a solid education, a community that helped raise us. But he also knew about the holes in my heart that Mom couldn't fill, no matter how hard she tried. There were deep, bottomless pools formed by abandonment and longing and an innate feeling of *never quite enough* and *a little too different.*

Back when I was young, I firmly believed that fancy clothes and a big house and a yard with a fence and a father who stayed would fill the dark, deep cavern I had inside that threatened at times to swallow me. And there was also a spirited rebel inside of me, one that longed to break free of what I perceived to be good and right and acceptable. I often found myself trapped between the rebellious fire that burned in my belly and the relentless need to be what everyone else wanted and expected me to be.

No wonder my dad didn't want to stay. I was a mess, unstable, unlovable, unbalanced.

"No, Katrina," Mom would assure me. "You've got it all wrong. Your dad loves you. He loves your sister."

"Then why isn't he here?" I asked, my voice more accusatory than inquiring.

My big sister, Candace, always gasped when I asked those kinds of questions. Candace took what was given to her, and she rarely asked for more. Candace was content, grateful, cooperative. She gasped, too, when my nine-year-old self called her a Penis Head in anger or frustration. And I called her a Penis Head often. I loved to shock her, to watch her react. She was a better girl than me in so many ways. She never questioned *why* or called me dirty names. At fifteen, she had a handsome boyfriend named Ryan, and she swooned over Sean Cassidy. She smiled a lot and took care of me when Mom was working. She made grilled cheese sandwiches and loaned me her VC Andrews books even though they were filled with arsenic-laced donuts and incest and other disturbing things that kept me awake at night.

Candace gratefully accepted what she had, never wanting more than she received. She was the content to my discontent; she was the calm to my storm. She was a gentler version of whatever blood ran through both our veins.

Our grandparents owned Park Lawn Cemetery in Evansville, Indiana, and Candace and I spent many sleepless nights in their magnificent, heavily windowed house nestled in between tombstones. There were corners of that house I could not visit, and I always averted my eyes when I walked up the stairs past the built-in bookcases that contained a dog-eared copy of *Rosemary's Baby*, a demon hand sticking out of a bassinet on the cover. In the daylight, I was brave, but when the shadows began to fall, my imagination took flight. Uncovered windows became portals into another world, where the living and the dead commingled.

"It's so peaceful," my mom would say. She would say the same thing when we walked without flashlights through the black-as-ink Brown County woods in the night. My mom was so brave, so bold. Nothing frightened her.

It's so terrifying, I would think. But I never said it out loud because I had an image to uphold, one in which I was just as strong as my warrior mom. And my youngest uncles were known for playing practical jokes—the kind that resulted in tears and an inability to sleep alone for at least six months. Fingernails scratching on locked doors, unexpected faces in the night, hands reaching up from under a bed once I was tucked in tightly with my cousins—those sorts of things. It was always safer, I thought, not to reveal my vulnerabilities.

I was both fascinated and horrified by the liminal spaces in my grandparents' cemetery, the threshold between the living and the dead. I was mostly intrigued, though, in the warmth of the sun and horrified when the moon made her appearance.

During the day, I'd walk from gravestone to gravestone, reading dates and studying etched pictures. As a child myself, it was the children's stones that most raptly held my attention. *How did she die? Was it an accident? An illness? How could tousled hair and skinned knees so easily turn to dust and dirt?*

"Be respectful of the dead," my grandpa would say, his handsome, chiseled face stern in the shadows of his office. "The graves are behind the stones," he explained. "Don't walk on them."

"Okay," I'd whisper with as much respect as I could muster. "I won't."

But I was a liar. There were some things I couldn't resist. And I couldn't resist lying down on the full-length slabs of concrete—the ones that covered the largest expanse of ground. I'd lie directly on the bones of another, hands folded across my chest, eyes closed to the sunlight. And I'd imagine what it might feel like to rest six feet underground, to have worms crawl through your eye sockets while maggots feasted on your skin. *Did it matter after you were gone? Did you leave your human body to walk among the clouds with saints and angels? Were the nuns right? Was there something else waiting after we were placed in the cold, dark ground for the rest of eternity? Did our souls elevate to something more? Something bigger? Something better? Was there a place where judgment ceased and everyone could be who he or she was made to be without fear of being outcast? Or were souls really thrown into the fiery depths of hell for lying, stealing, cheating, for coveting thy neighbor's wife, thy neighbor's girlfriend, thy neighbor's daughter, thy classmate with the long, red ponytail?*

One summer, my friend, Joy, and I planned to spend two weeks at Park Lawn with Grandma and Grandpa. A tornado hit the day before we arrived. Elderly, statuesque trees were uprooted, revealing remnants of what remained underneath, of what was once tangled in root and dirt.

Joy and I walked from unexpected hole to unexpected hole, peering tentatively into the damp dirt below, gruesomely identifying bits of bone and human, speaking in hushed whispers out of respect and fear.

Go. Go, I thought, speaking to the souls of the departed, to those inhabited by worms and roots. Go while you have the chance. Fly away. And I imagined spirit souls swirling around me, some jubilant, some scared, some sad. What did it feel like to experience the earth and sky a second time when all your vacant eyes had seen for so long was the deep, dank dark?

"I never want you girls to be buried in the ground," my mom promised. "I'll make sure you have crypts before I go."

Grandpa once showed me how caskets were placed into the hollow, dark caverns in the mausoleum.

"We use ball bearings to make the caskets slide in more easily," he explained.

I thought about the ball bearings in my roller skates—the ones I sported every fourth Friday at Goff's roller rink. The ones that supported my dance moves when "My Sharona" and "Centerfold" were played over the loudspeakers. The ones I wore when I dreamt guiltily about how it might feel for that gorgeous and popular eighth grader, Angela, to kiss me in the coatroom, her Dr. Pepper Lip Smackers mouth meeting mine, her Love's Baby Soft lingering on my skin.

It would break my mother's heart to know—many unknown things would break my mother's heart—but I didn't want to spend eternity in a crypt. Grandpa locked the mausoleum at night, and it felt like a trap. I never wanted to be contained. Those poor souls, tucked inside a too cold prison all day and night, unable to feel the sun or taste the rain. The ground seemed much more alive with its earthworms and leaves and organic soil.

Although it was a mortal sin within the confines of Catholicism—the religion that molded and formed the essence of me—what I really wanted was to be cremated, for the ashes of my remains to be scattered in my favorite places, in my favorite untouched places. Brown County. The Boys Club. The St. Michael's kickball diamond. Uncle John's backyard pool. The field behind our apartment building. I wanted to become part of what made me, to complete the circle. I wanted to be free to ride the winds that lifted and carried me to places I'd not yet seen: New York City, London, Dublin, Tuscany, Paris. I wanted a speck of me to fall on the Eiffel Tower in case I never made it there on my own.

I did not want to be an etched-in-stone picture girl. A reminder that I was here and then I wasn't. A monument to what was instead of what could have been. I wanted to be earth, wind, and water. I wanted to live forever in the elements. I wanted to say, "Here I am," instead of, "I once was."

I did not want to be forgotten.

* * *

Cecilia poured me a glass of wine, and we planned our two-day adventure in Manhattan. Bloody Marys and avocado toast at Balthazar, shopping in SoHo, dinner at Raoul's.

"We have a 2:00 with Alex," she said.

"Is Alex someone I should know?" I asked.

"Of course! Alexander Wang! Balenciaga! My favorite designer!"

I was not really into the fashion scene, but I knew he was a pretty big deal. I was already anxious about my size 12 body in a size 2 store, not to mention the $1,000 clothes on my $10 budget.

My body, my clothes, my looks—I can't really recall a time when I wasn't self-conscious about all of them. The best and worst part of my childhood existence was undeniably my cousins' hand-me-downs. They came to us in Blocks and Lazarus shopping bags—the kind with the sturdy bottom and the plastic handles, the kind that Kmart didn't provide, not even for the famous Blue Light Specials. The bags were exciting enough, but the clothes. Oh, the clothes! When they arrived, it was like a Christmas we'd imagined, but never experienced. Mom, Candace, and I would gather in the living room and pull each item out, piece by piece.

"I want to try that one!" Candace said.

"That one's mine!" I yelled in return.

Even Mom claimed a shirt here and there.

Candace and I grabbed and threw things and ripped those beautiful, sturdy bags. More often than not, I ended up in tears.

Many times, there were tags still attached to the items. It made me feel almost dizzy, this notion. I imagined a life in which I could walk into a fancy department store and choose dresses that I may or may not ever wear. Touching the fabric, running my hands along the details of each article, tracing the buttons made me heady. The bags of clothes were filled with girly colors and frilly hems, a far cry from my cutoff jean shorts and tank tops. For those brief moments, I lived another life. It was a mini-vacation when our department store bags arrived, an inexpensive trip to a place we couldn't afford to visit.

The reality, however, was that I could wear very little of the treasures we received. My skinny cousins were long and lean and beautiful, and I was athletic and sturdy. Jeans didn't button, zippers didn't close. The hand-me-down days were an exercise in emotions—from sky high to despondent. But I still claimed some of those things as my own. I hung them on my side of the closet, way in the back so Candace would forget about them. I'd take them out from time to time and admire them. I'd imagine what it would feel like to slough off my tomboy clothes and dress like a girl for once. Heels and ribbons and bows at my neck. I'd run my fingers over the still-attached tags and wander the brightly lit department store aisles in my fantasies.

* * *

When we arrived at his flagship store in SoHo, Alex came from the back to greet Cecilia. He was small, dark-haired, clad in black. The angles of his cheeks were sharp and stunning; his gender-fluid presentation, mesmerizing.

"Hello, Cecilia," Alex said quietly, embracing her in a familiar hug. "It's nice to have you back."

Cecilia hugged him with her long, lean arms. "It's always so good to be back!"

"Hey, beautiful, so good to see you again!" one of the employees exclaimed.

"Cecilia, you look amazing as always!" said another.

"Thanks, loves," she said, kissing each of their cheeks. "This is my friend, Katrina. She's a famous author."

"Oh," The employees both replied before they immediately turned back to Cecilia and Alex. No one asked me a question or spoke to me again. *Maybe they just weren't into books*, I thought. *Authors were of no interest to them. Surely I wasn't being dismissed because of my thick thighs and my Old Navy leggings. Could they tell by sight they were from Old Navy? Could they see in my eyes that I couldn't afford anything they had to offer? Was it the way I walked? The way I carried myself?* I perched self-consciously on the long, low, leather couch while Alex and Cecilia talked about some of his new designs.

After a few awkward moments of sitting alone with a pit in my stomach and my cheeks burning, I stood up to look through a few of the items hanging near me. A $400 turtleneck here, $700 riveted pants there. I eyed a trench coat that was edgy and fun and gulped at the $1,600 price tag.

You don't belong here, I thought to myself. *You are out over your skis. You need to learn your place.*

I felt just like I did when I was six and hiding in a closet with my sister and three of my wealthy cousins. My mom was babysitting while my aunt and uncle enjoyed an Alaskan cruise, and Mom was investigating a strange noise downstairs. Candace, my cousins, and I were huddled together, waiting to hear whether the coast was clear or whether we were all going to meet an early demise.

"Don't worry," one of my cousins said as we sat in the dark, her voice quiet and comforting. "You and Candace are safe. Kidnappers only want the rich kids."

"I've got one like that," Cecilia said, sidling up beside me and snapping me out of my childhood memory. "If you want it, you better grab it now because once they're gone, they're gone."

"Ha!" I said. "I think you're overestimating my net worth. If I spent that much money on one item of clothing, my kids wouldn't eat for months!"

"You only live once," she said. "You're going to be rich and famous someday. You should start acting—and dressing—like it."

"I'll act like it when I'm actually rich and famous," I said, rolling my eyes and trying to act cool. "And I couldn't fit my big toe into these clothes."

"You will when I'm finished with you," she said. "Stop eating so much shit and try something green for once."

I glanced sideways to see if anyone had heard her, and then I walked away—trying to feign nonchalance—to hide my feelings of shame and embarrassment. I had grown used to Cecilia's cutting comments about my weight and my eating habits, but that didn't mean they hurt any less. Cecilia was the queen of the hug/slap. She'd boost my ego one second, then cut me to my core the next.

"No one in your life has ever been this honest with you," she said. "You're just not used to it. True friends wouldn't have let you gain so much weight. Your husband shouldn't have. Everyone else enabled you, but I'm not into that feel-good bullshit. You can thank me later for saving your health."

There was nothing to say to her when she made these kinds of remarks. She wouldn't back down no matter what I said in return, and she would never, ever apologize. She never saw the need. Defending myself or calling her out on her bullshit would result in a nasty fight, and the fighting just wasn't worth it to me. Not when I had so little time with her. I was willing to tolerate her mean, condescending side to bask in the sunshine of her magnetism and charm.

I noticed that people stopped and stared when we walked the streets of SoHo together. She was so tall, stunning, impeccably dressed, confident.

"People sometimes think I'm a trans woman because I'm so tall," she told me once. "And sometimes, they think I'm Sandra Bullock. I like to keep them guessing."

She was loud and boisterous and occupied every bit of her surrounding space. She was generous with the unhoused, slipping them large bills and buying them shoes and socks to replace their worn, ragged footwear. In her signature hats and designer sunglasses, I'm certain people thought she was someone famous. I'm pretty sure she thought she was famous, too. Self-confidence like that goes a long way.

There were moments I got so lost in her that I forgot she was simply a flawed and imperfect human, too. There were times I thought myself unworthy of her attention and love. And there were moments like this that I'd do anything to spend a small number of precious, electric hours with her.

* * *

A few months after that whirlwind trip to New York, winter was settling in, and I drove to Cecilia's Parkersville cottage with a requested bottle of Cabernet that had taken my bank account down to double digits. She had a fire crackling in her antique wood stove and cozy blankets on the couch. Her dogs were all gathered around her as I made my way in. I no longer knocked at her house. We were well beyond that common courtesy.

Her kids were at their dad's for the night, and she already had an open bottle. I poured myself a healthy glass and joined her on the couch.

"It took you long enough to get here!" Cecilia teased. "I'm already half a bottle in!"

"Don't worry, I'll catch up," I said. "I'm a speed drinker."

"Oh, I know! I've seen you in action!"

We laughed and drank and talked about everything and nothing. She played some new songs for me on her laptop, and we snuggled together so we could both see the screen. We watched an SNL skit that she'd missed, and we emptied our glasses. I got up to pour us more, and she followed me into the kitchen.

In an instant that felt like an entire lifetime of fear, anxiety, longing, and lust, she pulled my head to hers and kissed me long and slow. When her tongue parted my lips to meet mine, I went weak with desire. She ran her fingers through my hair with her right hand and pulled me even closer with her left. I wrapped my arms around her and ran one hand up and down her spine, gently feeling the gentle bends of every vertebra. As we kissed, I felt her left hand at my waist, then gasped as she slid that hand into my leggings.

She whispered into my ear, "I guess I'm flippable."

Cool. Nonchalant. As if those four words didn't upend my entire existence.

Then she pulled back far enough for me to see that magic twinkle in her hazel eyes and her wicked, wild smile.

She led me to her bedroom and undressed me slowly. I watched, shivering, as she slipped out of her own clothes, her expensive lingerie, and pushed me gently onto the bed.

She led that night with gentle touches. With her words and her mouth and her requests. I would have done anything she asked. Her body was smooth and so incredibly soft under my hands, like butter. Her stomach, taut. Her legs, strong and muscled. I placed my hands on her hips, traced the delicious curves of her hip bones. She pulled my hands away, bound my wrists to the bed frame with satin ties, and touched every inch of my body. I moaned as she ran her hands up my thighs, further, further. I freed myself from the gentle knots and explored her with my fingertips, my eyes, my mouth. When she arched her back and came with my tongue on the most delicate part of her, I knew something within me had been forever changed.

We lay side by side when we were finished, and she ran her finger casually along my arm.

"Girl, you cannot tell me you're not experienced with women," she said.

"Only once," I said. "A long, long time ago. Just once."

"Well, you could have fooled me," she laughed.

"I mean, I *am* a woman. That makes me pretty familiar with what might feel good."

She kissed me again and pulled back abruptly.

"What's wrong?" I asked.

"Nothing at all!" she promised. "I just had a great idea. I've booked our ski resort in Michigan the first weekend in January, but the kids can't go because they'll be with their dad. Let's go together!"

"I've never skied before," I said.

"It will be a blast! You're an athlete—you'll love snow skiing!"

"I'm scared of heights, you know," I said. "Maybe I'll just sit by the fire in the lodge with a book."

"Oh, my God," Cecilia said, rolling her eyes. "You're such a pussy. We're going on a ski trip, not a reading trip."

And so I agreed. Because I agreed to everything she proposed, to everything she brought into my life, to every adventure we could possibly share.

I approached Charles apprehensively the next day. "I'd really like to go on this ski trip with Cecilia," I said. "It's just a long weekend. We'll be back late on Sunday."

"Well, that's the weekend Scott goes back to UC," Charles said.

"I know," I said. "But you were planning to drive him on Saturday, anyway, right?"

"I suppose," Charles sighed. "Do what you want, Katrina. I'll take care of things here."

I chose not to see the pain in his eyes, to hear the hurt in his voice. I absolved myself of feeling guilty about missing Scott's last two days at home—he'd probably spend them with his friends, anyway. I wanted nothing but Cecilia. She was every thought, every breath, everything.

She once said to me, "When we move to Colorado together, we'll grill in the backyard and drink a lot of really good wine. You'll write books, and I'll build a Pilates empire. We'll travel to New York and Tinder up all the beautiful boys. We'll have each other and a boy on the side now and then." The possibility of such a life drove me mad with longing. The promise. The tease. Even if it included boys on the side and not just me.

As the ski trip approached, Cecilia grew distant. I asked her about details, departure times, what to pack. She hemmed and hawed and talked about needing to visit her brother soon. I bought ski pants, a jacket, and gloves. I Googled photos of the Michigan resort, swathed in white lights. It was magical.

I asked Cecilia about our departure again.

"Stop asking me, Katrina!" she said, irritated and short. "I might not even go. And if I do, when I leave is none of your business."

I was shocked into silence as she spoke about *her* trip, about *her* plans. Did she forget that she'd invited me?

"Things change," she said. "Sometimes you just have to adjust."

Her words and her demeanor could flip in an instant, from kindness and warmth to cold, angry indifference. She was a speeding car that jolted to an unexpected stop. She was a gale force wind that whips up out of nowhere and snaps your beautiful kite in half.

By the time the Thursday of our planned weekend trip rolled around, she was no longer speaking to me at all. When I drove to the high school to pick up my kids, I saw her Land Rover headed North, her Thule loaded on top, and I knew she was going without me.

For two days, my mind swirled with confusion. By Friday night, I kept wondering if she was going to call and tell me to meet her. I felt crazy, unhinged. I kept my calendar free, hoping for that last minute re-invitation. I hated the weakness of my inaction, of my inability to confront her with what she had done.

"This is who she is," Charles said. "We all know it. I'm sorry that she's hurt you, but you can't expect her to be human. Cecilia doesn't care about anyone but Cecilia. And her kids. That's it. That's all she's capable of."

I didn't believe him. Didn't want to believe him. She'd stroked my hair gently as we'd kissed. I'd felt every inch of her body. We'd talked about our future together, raising kids, traveling, creating our separate empires, but together. She'd told me she'd loved me more than anyone she'd ever loved. There had to be a misunderstanding. I chose to drive Scott back to college on Saturday. I reveled in those last moments of time we had together before his spring semester began. We talked about football and basketball and home brewing. I dropped my firstborn freshman off on campus, and my heart was wrung out all over again. Leaving him was never easy. Our lives were so different when Scott wasn't around, the family dynamic irrevocably changed.

"I love you, Mom," he said as he grabbed his clean laundry.

"I love you, too, Scotty J.," I said. "Have a great semester!"

As I started to drive the three hours home, night began to fall. Small snowflakes clung to my windshield, and my chest heaved with sobs. Leaving him while being left by her was too much.

I pressed her number on my phone, listened to her voicemail greeting.

"Hey, it's me," I said. "I just dropped Scott off, and I'm already missing him. Missing you, too. I don't know what happened, but I wish I was with you. Call me if you can. I'll be in the car for another couple of hours."

But as strongly as I willed it to come, there was no return call. Just a cold, empty silence in the car as I logged the miles back to our Parkersville house, my entire body aching with the pain of her rejection.

On Monday, the call finally came. I saw her name on my phone, and my heart leapt out of my chest.

"Hello," I said hesitantly, not wanting to seem too eager.

"Hey!" she said. Her voice was full of life and joy. "We're having the best time! The snow has been perfect, and we've been skiing day and night. But there was a huge snowstorm today, and travel is slow. I don't think I'm going to make it back in time to pick the kids up from school. Do you mind grabbing them and running them home?"

My mind was reeling. *We? She wasn't alone?*

"Sure," I said. "Do they know I'm coming?"

"They're expecting you!"

Of course she'd already told them I would bring them home. She knew I wouldn't say no. I would have done anything for her, anything to keep her, anything to prove my love and devotion, anything to stay front and center in her life. I had lost myself in her, and I couldn't find my way back out. I was appalled by my own weakness, my dependence on her. And yet, in that moment, I was powerless to change it. And the most degrading and devastating part? I didn't want to change it.

"Thanks, love!" she said. "I owe you one!"

I hung up the phone and felt the punch in my gut. The realization washed over me, knocked me off my feet. She was there with her Russian lover. I'd suspected it, but now I knew for certain. The two of them hadn't spoken for months, but when he came back, she always moved heaven and earth to be with him. She could not resist the pull of him, the allure of him, no matter how much they hurt—and would continue to hurt—each other. I understood that kind of desperation. She'd taken our ski trip and turned it into their romantic getaway instead. She'd replaced me with him, and she didn't even have the decency to tell me. She'd left me wondering, guessing, sitting by the phone in case she called and told me to come. But she had never intended to call. I was her back-up plan. But even worse, I had let myself be her back-up plan.

After I dropped her kids at her house, I took my ski pants, jacket, and gloves back for a refund. The tags were still attached.

CHAPTER 4

"Have you had sex with her yet?" Charles asked one Tuesday evening after the kids had gone to bed. We were sitting in our respective chairs in the family room, reading and drinking. It was an evening I wasn't going to Cecilia's, but not by choice. She'd called earlier to tell me she was tired and going to bed early. That could have meant she was seeing her Russian lover. It could have meant she'd found someone new on Tinder. It could have simply meant she actually was tired. With Cecilia, I never knew for sure.

I hesitated. Took a deep breath. Felt my heart race a little. Bookmarked Hanya Yanigihara's *A Little Life* and laid it purposefully on my lap.

Then I looked at his face.

"Yes," I said. "Just once."

He was silent for more than a moment.

As his silence stretched into discomfort, I thought about my sophomore year in college, Charles's freshman year, when I had transferred from IU to Ball State University. Charles had received a scholarship, and we had grown weary of the effort it took to sustain our long-distance relationship. It seemed like the next logical step. And so, I left the place I loved so well to join him in Muncie, Indiana. I loved him, too. It seemed like a small sacrifice.

I roomed that first year with Joy, my old grade school friend. And as a junior, I got my own apartment, a single. I enjoyed the solitude, a quiet place to re-group. I'd joined a sorority and spent many daylight hours with my sisters—a bonding concept I'd been wary of before, but embraced when I met some amazing friends. In the evenings, I relished the chance to read quietly, to write my essays alone, with only my thoughts and ideas to keep me company.

Night running had become my favorite form of unwinding after long college days filled with exams and assignments and social expectations. It cleared my thoughts, calmed my nerves. And after an otherwise ordinary late night run, with my mind on an endorphin high, I didn't even notice the man behind me.

He caught the outside apartment door—the one I'd just unlocked—with his foot, this stringy-haired, pale stranger. I barely glanced at him as I wiped the sweat from my eyes and turned the volume down on my Sony Walkman. It had been a good run—fast, fierce—and I was ready to shower and head to bed.

I walked to the elevator. He followed.

"Which floor?" I asked, ready to push the button, always the good girl, the helpful girl. I looked at him as the elevator door closed—really looked—and saw the darkness in his eyes.

"Yours," he said, revealing the shiny knife in his hand.

The elevator shut with finality, and my heart dropped to the floor.

How did I get away? Could I run as soon as the doors opened? Would he be faster than me? Did I scream? Knock on all my neighbors' doors as I raced down the hallway? Did I kick him? Wrestle the knife from his rough-knuckled hands? What could go wrong? What could go right?

I was a strong girl, a former three-sport athlete. Every fiber of my being told me to either fight or to flee fast.

But when the elevator doors opened, I walked obediently to my apartment door, unlocked it. Silent. Submissive. Frozen within my own body, paralyzed in my own mind.

I found out I was not a fight girl. I was a flight girl. And I flew somewhere safe inside my mind and body.

The next moments of time—*were they minutes, hours, days?*—come back to me in hazy shadows, a black and white film noir played in an empty theater.

Blood, regret, bargaining, remorse.

Please, God, let me live. Despite all my transgressions, please let me stay. I will be good. I will be good. I will be good.

Threats, zippers, grunts, semen, a thousand little deaths.

"Do you want to die tonight?" he asked.

"No," I whispered, my voice unrecognizable. "Please, no." I begged him, submitted to him, acquiesced.

He turned my head to the side and held it there with his arm so I could no longer see him. The physical pain was searing. First his fingers, then his penis, hard and insistent. My body resisted, my flesh tore. Eyes wide open, cheek smashed to the floor, I could see the stains on my apartment carpet, could smell the residue of past residents in the fibers.

There was where I spilled the Purple Passion.

Here was the milk stain from the Froot Loops.

Framed pictures of family and friends watched from their cheap end table homes, from their plastic Kmart frames.

Look away, I begged silently. *Close your eyes.*

Charles left a voicemail message while this dirty stranger was on top of me.

"Hey, it's Katrina. I can't come to the phone right now, so leave me a message!"

Beep.

"Kat, it's me. I keep falling asleep trying to write this paper, so I'm going to bed now. Hope you had a good run. Love you."

Beep.

I floated above myself, up, up, up, suspended in time, watching the violent night below. My wings kept me suspended, wings I didn't even know I possessed until that moment. Soul disassociated from body. Rising. Like a butterfly. A Phoenix.

Ceiling Girl.

"Stay right here for thirty minutes. Do not scream. Do not call the police. I will kill you. Know that I always can."

His voice was low, full of gravel and anger and insistence.

I did not scream.

For twenty-five years, I did not scream. I'd forgotten how. I whispered instead, fearful of my own voice, unwilling to claim my own power and place in this world. This was my second lesson in remaining silent, in acquiescing, in trying to be the good girl—to do the right thing—to counterbalance the bad thing.

When the stranger left with his semen between my legs and his face stamped onto my brain, I showered and scrubbed and tried to erase every bit of him from my existence. But he was there forever, indelibly. Despite the scalding water. Despite the full bar of soap. Despite the skin I rubbed raw with my bright blue, 2-for-1 washcloth from JCPenney.

I broke up with Charles the next day.

"I just need a break," I said. "I think we need a break."

He was surprised, but he didn't argue, didn't try to win me back, didn't ask questions. Instead, he found his way into Monica Lewis's pants while we were apart.

He didn't know, of course. Couldn't have known. There was no blame to place, but I needed to place some blame. And he'd run so quickly to Monica. I told him about the rape later, once we'd reunited. He'd cried and apologized and begged forgiveness for not being there for me. But I couldn't shake the image of Monica from my mind, his hand in her pants, her tongue in his mouth. I imagined myself curled into a ball on my Babar comforter, crying into my pillow, trying to disappear into myself as they moaned and kissed and came. Their physical pleasure eclipsing my corporeal nightmare.

Betrayal after betrayal.

A stranger's.

Charles's.

Mine.

* * *

"You told me to have a girlfriend if that's what I needed, Charles," I said. "I'm trying to figure out what's going on inside me."

"What did the sex feel like to you?" he asked. "Was it better? Different?"

I sighed and looked out the patio door at the glow of the moonlight on the pond. I didn't want this to be a contest or a battle. The truth is, though, that sex with Charles—or any man before him—had never felt quite right. There was always a disconnect for me. I had tried being physical with numerous men in high school and a few in college, and I'd hoped that someday it would feel right, that something would click within me. But heterosexual sex was more of a perfunctory, performative act than anything I actually wanted. I had long thought my hesitation might have been born out of my Catholicism and the guilt that was inherently associated with sex for pleasure instead of procreation. With Cecilia, though, there was nothing I wanted more. When her body was with mine, it just felt right. Once I'd experienced it, I craved her skin, her lips, the touch of her fingertips, the feel of her long hair brushing my body.

"It was different, for sure," I said.

"You've never really enjoyed sex with me, have you?" he asked. "Have you always just considered it part of the marriage contract?"

"It's complicated, Charles," I said. "I love you. I do. And this confusion is not about you specifically. But what I feel for Cecilia is different. I can't explain it. I'm trying, but I'm not there yet."

"Why her?" he asked. "What's the draw? She's not even very nice to you."

"I don't know," I said. "I truly don't. But it's all-consuming. I go to bed thinking about her. I wake up thinking about her. It's not anything I consciously chose. It just is. But I have to figure it out. Otherwise, it's always going to be sitting there between you and me."

We talked about my propensity to form unusually strong female bonds, to dive headfirst into my closest relationships. I thought long and hard about one of my best friends in high school and how jealous I became when she chose another friend and turned our duo into a trio. I recalled my girlhood crushes on summer camp counselors who occupied more than their fair share of space in my head. I reminisced about a female high school teacher whose after-school classroom became my daily destination, a space that I craved intensely so I could spend more time with her, confide in her, simply exist in her orbit.

"Does this feel different than friendship? With or without the sex?" he asked.

I nodded, even though I couldn't quite articulate why. Charles then confronted me with the biggest question of my life.

"Are you gay?" he asked.

The word hung in the air between us. It was hard to think about, challenging to consider. I'd grown up in a world where gay was not really an option. Or at least not a desirable one. My Granny used to call our local TV star, Cowboy Bob, "Gay Bob" because she mistakenly believed that was his name. And we all thought it was hilarious. Gay was funny. Gay was foreign. Gay was whispers and giggles behind backs. Gay was a slur. Gay was a hard word for me to say at all, let alone in reference to myself. Lesbian was even harder. Queer was so offensive that Candace and I weren't allowed to say it when we were young, so we called each other "quee" instead.

"I don't know," I said to Charles as I began crying. "I joined this secret online group of late-in-life lesbians, and someone there said that if you're questioning this much, then you're gay, because straight women don't stay awake at night wondering if they're gay. That's all I can think about now. So, what does that mean?"

"Kat," Charles said, "We've both known that you have some same-sex leaning tendencies. You've had some pretty high-intensity friendships. You've admitted to me before that you found them all attractive."

"But isn't it normal for women to have strong connections like that?" I asked. "Isn't that part of the difference between women and men? The whole Mars and Venus thing?"

"Were you physically attracted to them?" Charles asked.

I thought for a moment.

"Well, yes," I said. "But they're attractive women."

"I think Brad Pitt is a handsome dude, Kat. But I'm not physically attracted to him," Charles said.

I'd never really thought about splitting the hairs between finding someone attractive and being sexually attracted to someone. But there was definitely a difference.

"What do you feel about Cecilia?" Charles asked. "What do you want from her?"

I didn't know how to answer him then, how to help him understand. I only knew how much I desired Cecilia's company, her presence, her touch. I was enamored with her, trapped within the aura of her, couldn't get enough. She created a want within me that I could barely contain.

How did I convey to him that I wanted her to read me like a beloved book, pages dog-eared and soft with use. I wanted her to know my story, the unspoken nuances. I wanted her to ponder them as she lay in bed at night, golden hair fanned out beneath her head, long legs tangled within the sheets.

I wanted coffee stains on my cover in the morning and an earthy wine wiped from the paragraph she couldn't stop reading by the evening fire. I wanted her to return again and again to her favorite passages, ingesting them, memorizing them, until she could no longer recall whether they were pieces of her or pieces of me.

I wanted her to run her finger along the spine of me, softly, lovingly, outlining my title with her slender finger until she knew the feel of it by heart. I wanted her to fall asleep with my pages open on her chest so I could feel the rise and fall of her every breath, to softly ride the life within her.

My desire for her consumed me, and I did not look back to see what I might be leaving in my wake—the churning waters, the unsettled seas, the waves lapping at every foundation. The beautiful blue horizon loomed before me, and I could focus only on that. On the possibility. On the dream. I could only see the sunshine while the storm clouds formed at my back.

* * *

"I think we should consider counseling," Charles said a week later. I could tell he was struggling as much as I was, but in different ways. He seemed lonely, withdrawn. Outside, our lives looked familiar—visiting Scott at UC, attending the kids' choir and orchestra concerts, hosting friends for weekend gatherings—but nothing about our relationship was the same. We were distant with each other, careful. We were standing on the edge of a cliff, looking into the abyss, our legs shaking with fear.

"I think that's a good idea," I agreed.

"I think it's the only way to save this marriage," he said. "That is, if you still want to be in this marriage."

"Charles, please don't say that," I said. But in my heart, I knew there was some truth in what he was brave enough to speak.

"You need to figure out who you are," he said. "If you're bisexual, we can make it work. If you're gay, we can't. It's pretty simple." That was Charles. Black and white. Cut and dried. No shades of gray for him, while a smoky charcoal was where I tended to exist.

"Nothing about this is simple," I told him. "But I want to go to counseling with you. I want to work through this with you."

He found a marriage counselor that our insurance covered, and within a week, we were sitting on opposite sides of Laurel's orange couch, a full cushion in between us. After numerous arguments that ended in silent nights, back-to-back in bed, Charles and I were both nervous and guarded. Laurel positioned herself in a chair across from us, leaning forward, her forearms on her knees. The room was dark, with brown accents and gold fixtures. End tables held lamps with dim lights and tissues. It had been a while since I'd sat in a counselor's office, and I forgot how vulnerable and small it made me feel. It was almost the same feeling I had in Catholic confessionals as a child, exposed and raw and afraid of the judgment to come.

"Thank you both for being here today," Laurel said. "It's a testament to your marriage that you're both willing to take this step. Who would like to tell me a little about where you are?"

Charles, of course, spoke up instantly. Speaking was his forte, his day job. I listened as he talked about Cecilia and said words like gay, lesbian, bisexual, lonely, abandoned, soulmate, and wedding vows.

When it was my turn, my words included confused, guilty, afraid, religion, suffocated, unsure, and unraveling.

"You might be two of the most self-actualized people I've had the pleasure of working with," Laurel said. "I can tell how much you care about each other, and I can also understand why this crossroads is so difficult for you both. But I feel confident we can work through this together to reach whatever resolution you both want and need."

Laurel sounded far more confident than I felt. In my mind, our situation was unprecedented, untenable, impossible.

As Charles began to go into detail about how lonely his evenings were and how much he missed me, I went from feelings of guilt and sadness to feelings of anger and defensiveness.

"But you have to understand, Laurel, that I've sacrificed a great deal for Charles over the years," I said. "I raised our four kids while he worked on two advanced degrees, I moved our family 500 miles away from everything we'd ever known when he decided he needed a career change, and I agreed to his 50% pay cut because I knew his job was killing him. I haven't asked for much in this marriage, and I just want a little time to spend with Cecilia to figure myself out."

"When I said to go find a girlfriend, I also said that I wanted to be involved," Charles said. "And what's currently happening is 100% just you and Cecilia."

"How do you want to be involved?" I asked. "What does that mean? Do you want to have sex with her?"

"Not necessarily," he said, although I could tell by his voice that the option wasn't off the table for him. "I just want to be included. I want to be invited over to hang out with you sometimes. You're traveling with her to places I wanted to take you."

"But you haven't taken me," I said. "If you wanted to travel so badly, why aren't we traveling?"

"Because there's never any money," Charles said. "You spend it all."

"I spend money on groceries and things for the house and clothes and activities for the kids," I said. "It's not like I'm dripping in diamonds or wearing designer clothes. What are you accusing me of?"

"You always want more," he said. "Bigger houses, newer cars, modern furniture. You resented the fact that I took a 50% pay cut when I changed jobs. You've never forgiven me for that. You have to admit, Katrina, you have never been a gentle breeze."

And on and on we went, sifting through twenty-two years of marriage and twenty-nine years of partnership, digging through all the detritus of our past, all the missteps, all the misunderstandings. We held it like dirt in our hands, let it sift through our fingers, as the sharp, jagged edges of all the wrongs we'd ever wrought made themselves known. Then we threw those pieces at each other with little regard for how much they might cut, how much they might hurt. We didn't care about the mess we left at our feet. We dug in and smashed those bits of dirt into the carpet. Laurel interjected here and there until our time was up. When we left that day, nothing had been resolved, but everything had been laid bare.

And that was just the beginning.

CHAPTER 5

I sat on the balcony above Howard Street in SoHo, and the dark heat settled on my shoulders like a blanket, warm and damp. It was not altogether comfortable, not necessarily uncomfortable. But I wore it like a jacket loaned on a chilly night, even though I wasn't in need of comfort or warmth. It was a gift, and so I accepted it, wrapped myself up in it, felt the itch of the collar around my neck and turned it into a caress instead. Everything given can be a gift, really, depending on how you see it. If you choose to notice the shine instead of the stain.

Cecilia and I were in New York City with our daughters for the weekend. It was supposed to be a trip for the two of us, just she and I. But there was a street fair with a *Girl Power* theme happening, and she decided her daughter, Chloe, should be here, too. Because she decided, because this is her place, because she so graciously offered her home up to us, I brought my Marley as well, so the teens could enjoy the city together.

Girl Power Times Two.

Cecilia was so connected to her daughter during those days, when oftentimes, mine could take or leave me. So, the dynamic felt a little different, a bit off-kilter. My daughter, SnapChatting and texting. Her daughter, searching for Pokemons and snuggling into her mother's neck.

But on this weekend, I couldn't help thinking, *Did she really want her daughter here, or did she just not want to be alone with me? Have we fallen too deeply into that uncomfortable space again? That friend or lover conundrum? That in-between?*

Or was I just hoping, wishing, that was the case? That she felt so much, she didn't know what to do with me?

She and I felt so differently.

On almost every level.

Me, wanting to be with her. She, craving the ebb and flow, which to me, feels like a necessary separation at best, an abandonment at worst. Because abandonment has always been my biggest demon, my abiding fear. And so I feel it like a ghost limb even when it's not real. Even when it's just a phantom in the recesses of my little-girl memory.

"You never cease to surprise me," I would say to her when unexpected words flew from her lips. And there was no greater truth about her. Her view of the world, her reaction to it, was so different from mine. Things that didn't necessarily bother me—a late arrival, service that wasn't quite up to par, a sideways glance taken the wrong way—could send her on a tirade. Her fire both fed and frightened me. I often tiptoed around things I wanted to say—things I needed to say—so I didn't say them the wrong way, so they didn't get misconstrued. "I think I know what you might say, and then I'm completely blindsided. Again and again and again," I would say, laughing.

"That's part of my magic," she would reply, running her fingers through her brand new, ultra-expensive cut, color, and lowlights.

She both balanced and kept me reeling—the best and worst—of all the emotions, of all the experiences.

I had been looking forward to this weekend with her and her alone. To talk, to ponder, to explore, to be. To maybe feel the softness of her lips one more time, the curve of her hip.

She said she wanted rest and relaxation. And then we brought the teenage girls. Which is glorious and lovely and special in its own way. But also, not necessarily relaxing. We spent our Friday running from place to place—favorite restaurants, new bookstores, tourist attractions—trying to meet the needs of four instead of two, planning for the few hours we had left in the city. If she and I had been here alone together, I would have been content to just exist beside her. Or in her proximity. No pressure, no plans, no expectations.

Just the being.

The being had been enough for me, had been so much.

After a long day of running and Ubering and sightseeing, the four of us returned to her SoHo apartment for a rest, with dinner reservations set for 8:00.

I took a quick, dreamy, late afternoon nap. Cecilia did the same in her own bedroom. My alarm went off at 7:15, and I showered, began getting ready for the evening. I could hear our girls doing the same.

At 7:30, Cecilia stumbled into the bathroom, groggy and grumpy, and said, "Take the girls to dinner. I'm too tired to do this. All week long, I'm ruled by my alarm clock and my to-do list. When I come here, I want to move at my own pace, to do my own thing, to sleep when I need to, to answer to no one."

And I was instantly angry.

Isn't that what we had planned? I wanted to yell. *Isn't that the long weekend we were going to spend together?* It was her idea to bring the girls, and now she was bailing on me. And I didn't want to fight in front of them, didn't want them to think they were any less important than our own needs and wants.

And so I agreed to take the girls to dinner and have her meet us there later.

And I fumed because I had wanted it to be just her and me from the get-go. From the start. An easy, sleep-in-till-noon getaway. She was the one who invited the chaos. And she's the one who relieved herself of the worry.

But then she arrived at Little Prince, just a few minutes late, in her short blue dress with her cute hat and her smiling eyes.

Those eyes.

And that smile.

And I was simply grateful to be there, in the mix of it all, whatever it was.

Whatever it might someday become.

Whatever it meant.

Or didn't mean.

* * *

No one filled, challenged, invigorated, exasperated, and illuminated me like Cecilia did. She was breath and life and death rolled up in a beautiful package of gentle skin and kaleidoscope eyes.

She was always up for an adventure, unless she was ready for a nap. She was ready to climb a mountain or dive off a Jamaican cliff, unless there was a rerun of "The Gilmore Girls" playing. She was the epitome of opposite ends of the spectrum, her downtime as important as her risk-taking.

As much as she moved me, Cecilia scared me. There was a volatility to her, an explosion simmering below the surface. Two ex-husbands, numerous ex-lovers, two lovely teenagers she adored and overindulged. One divorce decree that funded her extensive travel, her expensive homes, and her designer shoes. She was a mystery and an enigma wrapped in a cocoon of privacy. She'd give just enough to pull you in, then she'd slap you back where you belonged. Harshly. With zero remorse. Sometimes I'd text or say something to her—something I considered relatively benign, or kind, or funny—and she'd fire back with an unexpected, angry tirade. She misunderstood me often. Almost as much as she confused and intrigued and inspired me.

Cecilia made me want to be bigger than I was. She made me wish for a larger-than-life existence. And so I, too, bought Stuart Weitzman heels that I could not afford and regularly drank $75 bottles of wine to expand my palate.

When we were not together—when we were on opposite coasts or opposite sides of town—my missing her was a living, breathing thing, another entity that existed in my very marrow. It stopped me short when I least expected it. It stole the air right from my lungs, a nimble, greedy thief. I wanted to lean over and whisper something, to brush her cheek with my fingers, to inhale her laughter, to grasp her hair, her slender fingers.

She was a phantom limb to me, not there, but still there. Always there. An electric current that held me, burning, burning, in its grip.

I could not break free.

I did not want to break free.

But I wanted both of us to be free.

We would have withered and died, of course, without our wings.

I would not clip hers.

I would not clip mine.

The missing-her ache that sat in my chest was palpable, though. It doubled me over, a fist, a punch, an awakening.

It was hard, sometimes, to love her more than she loved me. That teeter-totter of imbalance kept me dizzy and unsure, the ground beneath me not quite solid, the horizon, heat-buckled.

I thought about her all the time, minute by minute, second by second. I had to shake my muddled head free of her, to stop myself from calling, from texting, from being too much.

I am so often *too much.*

Even for myself.

But the pull. The lightning. The magnet. It all upended me, turned me inside out. *She* upended me, turned me inside out. My guts splayed in every direction, my heart split in two, vulnerable to vermin and disease and destruction.

But for her, I took it. All of it. Accepted it. Embraced it. Ingested it.

Every bit.

That is what we do for our own bones, our own limbs, our own hearts beating wildly underneath pale skin, barely contained.

We choose to survive. We choose to feed what is hungry, to clothe what is naked, to warm what shivers, to soothe what aches, to staunch the bleeding, to cool the fever.

Self-sacrifice. Self-protection. Self-preservation.

Selfish.

Selfless.

I felt her—always, everywhere—floating on each breath, running through my veins, settling into my bones, making her home inside me where it had been patiently awaiting her arrival since the moment these lungs first expanded, contracted, expanded, contracted.

* * *

On one of our final adventures together, before everything inevitably began to crack at the seams, I visited Cecilia's apartment in New York City—a glorious, whirlwind forty-eight hours of a blue-sky weekend. When she threw open her window to introduce the city below, I first noticed the rust on the fire escape, the place where she'd posted online pictures the week before, the place where she'd slid easily into her new home, silkily, diaphanously.

I've always been embarrassingly afraid of heights.

"It's a physical reaction," I say to everyone who will listen, because I often feel an obsessive need to explain myself, to set the stage according to my own artistic vision. "Sweaty palms, full-body shaking. If my heart doesn't give in, I'm worried my balance will. Balance is something that matters when you're on the top of a precipice."

But I'm drawn to the dizzying summits, too—the rush, the challenge, the breathlessness.

Then I saw the drop below the rust. Four stories down, dirty concrete, luxury cars, bins of trash waiting to be collected.

Ten feet is a fatal fall, I heard my mother say in my head.

"Go on," Cecilia said. "Get out there. Don't be a pussy."

Then that crooked smile, half-wicked, half-kind. Half-endearing, half-terrifying. All breathtaking.

As I stepped out of the open window, the rust was rough on my bare feet, on my newly minted city blister. I wrapped my toes around the balcony rails, vaguely afraid of tetanus, but clinging, clinging, as if ten toes could save me from the drop.

As if anything could save me from this inevitability.

I stood, shaking, the hot night breeze wafting around me, lifting my shirt, and tossing my hair. Life bustled below, lovers fighting, shouts of *fuck you* and *no fuck you*, cars honking, flecks of decade-old paint and the detritus of harsh seasons—sun, wind, snow, rain—making the four story journey down to the street below, loosened by my wary, shaking bare feet.

"It's gorgeous," I said, blinking in the city lights, looking out but not down.

"Isn't it?" she said—a statement more than a question—stepping out to sit beside me. "There's the Empire State Building," she said, pointing.

Then she leaned in to kiss me, grabbing my ponytail, hard, and an electric jolt shot down my spine. I touched her face, the cottony softness familiar to my fingertips. I had felt it before, had missed and craved and desired it again. Her tongue was warm, my breath short. And when we parted, I noticed first the curve of her stunning smile, then the fleck of rust my hand had left on her face. I brushed it away gently, watched it begin its fall, four stories, down to Howard Street.

When I married my husband twenty-two years prior, we went to the Sierra Nevadas for our honeymoon. I was so excited about the gorgeous hiking, the great outdoors, the breathtaking views. I neglected to consider the correlation between mountains and the inevitable heights we would encounter.

We went hiking in Yosemite on our second day, jeans and sweatshirts and sturdy boots purchased just for the occasion. On our way to our intended waterfall view, we kept climbing up, up, up. Then we turned a corner on a path barely wide enough to walk side-by-side, and a dizzying drop—accompanied by a gorgeous view—was at our toes.

I plastered myself up against the mountain wall, shaking, crying, unable to move forward or back.

"Come on, Kat," my new husband said. "Hold my hand and close your eyes. I'll get you past this."

I couldn't breathe, couldn't move, couldn't function at any semi-reasonable level.

"Just go," I whispered. "Leave me here. I can't do it. I can't."

"Honey, don't be ridiculous. I just married you. I'm not going to leave you on the side of a mountain in California."

I often wonder now if he regretted not leaving me there that day. If his life would have been easier if he'd just hiked back down the mountain, leaving me to figure out my own fate. But somehow, some way, he got me back to the safety of flat land and then to the Napa wineries where I drank away any lingering fear.

And this memory—this honeymoon recollection—lodged in my brain as I watched that fleck of rust fall to the earth.

The two people I loved most in the world—one possibly willing to let me fall, to maybe even give me a push. The other—who I was convinced would never.

CHAPTER 6

I don't want to die alone.
I don't want to destroy my kids.
I don't want to destroy him.
I don't want to lose my friends.
I don't want to split the money.
I don't want to drive myself to the hospital.
I don't want to share holidays.
I don't want his family to hate me.
I don't want him to hate me.
I don't want to abandon anyone.
I don't want to be abandoned.
I love him.
I love her.
I love me.
It's beyond complicated.
But ...
I can't breathe.
I can't sleep.
I can't pretend any longer.
I have never been on my own.
I don't even know how to cook.
He has always taken care of me, lovingly, willingly.
Until I needed more space.
Then anger.
And hurt.

And resentment.
And *you said* and *no, you said* ...
And nothing is enough.
And it's all too much.
I'm too much.
He's too much.
She's too much.
We cared too little.
We held on too tightly.
We let go too often.
I ran away.
He ran away.
She always runs away.
So much running.
Too little breathing.
My lungs no longer work ... in and out, in and out.
Who am I?
Who is he?
Who is she?
What comes next?
What comes last?
Little deaths in the choosing.
Me.
Him.
Her.
Me.
Me.
Me.

CHAPTER 7

I'll admit I did not go into it easily. I was happy in Grand Haven, Michigan, vacationing with Cecilia, her kids, and my kids. We were there for four short, delicious days, sitting on a sunshine-soaked rented deck with cheese and crackers and the swell of our kids' laughter. There were decadent chocolates strewn throughout the house. The kids had discovered the local candy store and had befriended the owner. At least twice a day, they'd made their pilgrimage into town to buy more lavender truffles, more salted caramels. We'd all experienced skin rejuvenating face masks and purple-pink sunsets that disappeared into darkness too soon. I was sweaty and content and full of wine and laughter, and I didn't want to drive the four and a half hours to Charles's family reunion in Grayfield, our shared hometown. I wanted to stay and bask in the sun and not wash my hair and eat steaks cooked perfectly on the grill, my youngest son Jack's Tchaikovsky playlist wafting through the heavy air.

And so, as had become my modus operandi of late, I complained and procrastinated and then listened to bad 70s songs on the drive to Indiana to quell both my nerves and my dismay.

"Welcome! Welcome!" Pappaw exclaimed as we piled out of the car at the family farmhouse. The driveway was already packed. I'd been careful not to run over any of Pappaw's carefully tended flowers. He was a Master Gardener, and his landscaping was his pride and joy. The kids and I walked to the backyard where my niece and nephew had said their wedding vows a few years prior. The yard was in full bloom, and rented tables and chairs awaited our arrival under crisp, white tents. Pappaw poured me a glass of Cabernet and hugged me warmly. He'd been hesitant, distant when Charles and I first started dating, but in recent years, he and I had become much closer, sipping fine (and not-so-fine) wines and talking about the books we'd most recently read.

"So glad you're all here," he said as he patted my back, and the joy in his voice caused a rush of guilt to wash over me. Why had I felt any hesitation? These people loved and accepted me.

They were my family.

I chose a chair at an empty table, and several nieces and nephews gathered around, discussing their night-before antics and the resultant hangovers. My kids laughed and nodded, no doubt eagerly anticipating their own yet-to-come drunken escapades.

As the midday sun began to give way to evening, Charles came up behind me.

"Let's go to Greenie's for a drink," he whispered. "The kids are in good hands, and I'd love to catch up with you." It was our favorite place in town, the place where the bartenders knew which Cabernet was my first choice and that Charles preferred his Manhattan with Woodford Reserve. We were halfway through our first round of drinks when the fallout began, and the magical spell of the day was broken.

The conversation took a hard turn back to our shaky, damaged marriage, our questions about the future, our general unsteadiness, all the words we continued to skirt around but couldn't quite voice. *What do you want? What is your plan? What are you thinking? How are you feeling? When are you leaving? Why aren't you staying?* All of those questions became ammunition, and I fired back with pointed precision, cold, detached, impossible, angry. I was hard. I was ugly. I was impatient. I was not gracious with him when Cecilia was so deeply embedded in my heart. His questions—although he had every right to ask them—pushed me even further away. Answering them meant owning up to the destruction I was causing, and I was not ready to do that. Not then.

He drank the last of his Manhattan, we said goodbye to old high school acquaintances sitting beside us at the bar, and we walked back to the Navigator together, but not.

Our voices escalated in the privacy of our vehicle, and soon, I was fuming, yelling, accusing.

"You were the one who always wanted me more!" I screamed. "I was never given a chance to figure out what I wanted. You just pressured, pressured, pressured!" I was referring to our early courtship, when he asked me to go out with him multiple times, insistently, before I finally gave in and said yes. I was searching for something that would shift some of the blame to him, but I knew my arguments were flimsy and ridiculous. I was accusing him of loving me too much, unwilling to accept my own misgivings in the face of our marital strife.

"Jesus, Katrina!" he yelled back. "What are you even saying? What are you trying to say?"

"I'm saying that I feel trapped in a life that was never really my choice," I cried. "I did everything you wanted me to! I made you happy, had your kids, supported your career. I gave everything up for you!"

"What did you give up?" he yelled back. "A fatherless life? Poverty? Canned tuna for dinner?" His face was ugly with rage. "We created this life together! We chose this life together! I didn't force you into anything!"

Unwilling to take our vitriol back to his unsuspecting family members, we pulled into the soccer park where we'd once watched a cerulean-eyed, two-year-old Scott run and sweat and laugh, where we'd pushed a ginger, curly-haired Austin-imp in a double stroller, where I'd rubbed my swelling belly, full of Marley, and made all our plans for the future. It was there on those hallowed grounds we continued our never-ending, unrelenting, always-present fight.

"Do you want to stay in this marriage?" he yelled as I paced around the parking lot.

I didn't answer.

"Do you want to stay in this marriage?" he yelled again.

I didn't answer.

"Katrina, answer me, goddamnit!" he yelled again, his eyes bulging with anger, his hands balled into fists. "Do you want to stay in this marriage?"

I faced him, made steely-eyed contact even though my entire body was shaking, took a breath.

"I think we should separate," I said. "I think I want a divorce."

I had not yet spoken those exact words—the "D" word, the one we swore we'd never say unless we really meant it—and the wind was knocked right out of me, a rush of breath, a void in the space where my lungs a few minutes before were doing their dutiful job.

I had not said that word since I was twenty-five and we were fresh-faced newlyweds.

"I can't do this anymore," I'd screamed then at the man I'd recently married, when my face was young and void of wrinkles and there was no gray in my hair. "I don't want this life—this day in and day out of working and struggling and just barely getting by."

"Of course you don't," he screamed back. "You want the easy way out. You always have, and you always will! You want someone to come rescue you. *Poor Katrina with the father who left her.*"

His mention of my father had sent me into an uncontrollable rage. He always knew just where to stick his finger into my childhood wounds.

"Get out of this house!" I screamed. "GET OUT!"

"Where do you want me to go, Katrina?" he screamed back. "This is our home. This is what we both signed up for."

"I don't care where you go," I screamed. "I don't care what you do. I just want you GONE. NOW!"

He'd grabbed the keys to his truck and stormed out of the house, punching the wall as he went. His fist left a hole in the drywall. A forever reminder.

Our early marriage was tumultuous. Rocky. Volatile. We were young and poor and buried under the weight of bills and partnership and unknowns.

There were many fights—intense, all encompassing, loud, explosive.

"I think I want a divorce," I'd yelled, tears streaming down my face. "I think this was a mistake."

"Don't say that unless you mean it," he said. "Ever. Don't say that word."

"Divorce!" I yelled back. "DIVORCE! DIVORCE! DIVORCE!"

"God, you are such a baby!" he yelled at me. "Why don't you grow up and take some responsibility for your life?"

"Why don't you get OUT of my life?" I screamed back.

I needed someone to yell at. I was young and unsure about myself, about him, about us, about everything. We had mounds of bills, and I'd sit in the midst of all that paper and cry. He was a schoolteacher who didn't make much money. I had an entry-level corporate job and insurmountable student loan debts. It seemed we'd never get our heads above water.

"I can't do this," I'd cry. "We can't do this."

He'd respond to me with intensity and anger. He'd punch walls, windshields. But he never touched me.

Not then.

I was full of uncertainty and fear. He was the only man who had ever fully loved me. And I wasn't sure I was capable of loving him the way he needed to be loved.

Those days were exhilarating and exhausting and they drove me to the brink of madness.

I would get in the car and drive for hours at a time.

He stayed.

I wrote long, angry letters in red ink.

He stayed.

I did everything I could to convince him I was unworthy of his love and adoration.

He stayed.

I tried to convince him that I could not love him the way he needed to be loved.

He stayed.

I never truly believed I would be the one to go.

Until twenty-one years later when I said the "D" word again. And was afraid that I meant it.

"I'm sleeping at my mom's tonight," I said as I began to walk in the direction of my childhood home, less than a mile away from where we stood fighting. "Tell the kids. Or bring them there."

I stormed off in my favorite denim wedges, the sun on my back and a boulder in my throat.

With every step, I felt blisters forming on the soles of my feet. They grew and burned and reminded me pace after pace of the hurt I was creating, of the distress I was delivering to those I loved the most.

Charles followed me in the Navigator, yelled out the window, "I'm not leaving you here. Get in the car."

"I'm forty-fucking-six years old," I said. "I can walk three quarters of a mile to my goddamn house in broad daylight on my own. Go away."

"I know you're destroying your feet in those shoes," he said. "Get in the car."

But I was intent on destruction.

I stepped harder, harder, leaning into the fresh, tender spots of pain that were filling with pus and memory. And then the tears came, hot, angry, unexpected. They washed away my meticulously applied MAC Feline liner, my Lancôme mascara. Black streaks ran under my prescription sunglasses until they began to run clear. So many tears. So many.

Charles pulled out of the gas station where he'd been waiting for me.

"Katrina, you're so fucking stubborn sometimes. Get in the goddamn car."

The Cavalier behind him honked an impatient reminder that he was blocking turning traffic.

"Jesus Christ. Just go!" I said. "Leave my suitcase at my mom's."

When I turned into Bowman Acres—the neighborhood that had become my post-childhood-apartment home when Mom married my stepfather, Bruce, over a quarter of a century ago—I took off my heels and walked barefoot on the hot asphalt, blisters torn and bleeding and burning. Rocks sticking into tiny, intentionally created cracks and crevices of split skin. But I ignored the pain.

Instead, I looked at Allison's childhood house as I walked by. She was—and still is—my best friend, and she once lived a short block away from my high school home. Her parents had recently sold that house, and a different, younger family lived there now, as evidenced by the kids' plastic toys and sidewalk chalk strewn across the driveway. Another rush of tears came, hot, fast, choking. There we stood, under that tree, more than two decades ago in our matching Laurel Ashley jumpsuits, lamenting about unrequited love and Cs in Chemistry (mine, not hers), exchanging Flavia cards with sappy quotes and watercolor sunsets on the front. My always-there. The steadiest of my steadies. Even when she couldn't steady herself, she steadied me. She still does. Whenever I need her, I know she will be there, no matter our geography.

Then there was Uncle John's house. Uncle John, buried just a few months earlier, the first of the Applegate Eight to bid farewell. Our post-Grandpa family patriarch. Uncle John, who declined my invitation to the father/daughter Brownie dance because he didn't want me to be confused about the fact that he was my uncle and not my father. But I knew who my father was and who he wasn't. There was no confusion there. Uncle John, whose perfectly aqua backyard swimming pool always beckoned but remained unreachable behind a locked gate. Uncle John, the one I pined for and wanted and needed. Uncle John and his girls, his most beloved, his group of goddesses that—a bloodline a fraction too far away—would never include me.

I walked down Bowman Drive and remembered the hundreds of training runs I'd made in this very same place, dribbling with my right, then my left, then my right, then my left. Dribbling behind my back, between my legs, with my eyes closed. My basketball, merely an extension of my own ten fingers.

"A good ball handler is the opposing team's worst nightmare," Bruce had said time and time again. "No one should know you're left-handed. Keep them guessing."

Sobbing uncontrollably now, I turned into the driveway of my childhood home. Charles was there, unloading my overpacked weekend suitcase, silently wheeling it up to the front door where the wooden "Welcome" sign still hung, an old, weathered, friendly reminder of the old, weathered, friendly faces inside.

"I'll call you in the morning," Charles said. "Let me know when you head to the nursing home to see your mom."

Bruce must have heard the commotion because he opened the door as Charles walked away.

"Hey, Kiddo," Bruce said gently. "Welcome home. What are you doing here? Are you okay?"

"May I stay tonight?" I asked, tears and snot mixing into an unsavory mask. "Just a couch? Please?"

"Of course," he said. "This is your home. It will always be your home. And your bed is here, not just the couch."

I stepped across the threshold onto the familiar navy blue carpet, broken, confused, emotional, and safe in the arms of my beloved stepfather, the one who had always, without fail, without expectation, without need of anything in return, from the moment he said, "I do" to my mom, loved us all so well.

CHAPTER 8

I am not in love with you.

This is what she wrote to me after one more late night filled with wine and discussion and contemplation. It was buried deep in between the lines of what she did feel about me, how much she loved me, how much she cared for us, how she wanted us to be together forever, as friends.

In between the lines.

The phrase took on new meaning when her email illuminated my phone in the middle of the night.

It broke me clean in two.

Those seven words were all I could see. Those seven shifted everything, threw shade into all my sunny places, cut straight into the beating heart of me.

I am not in love with you.

I could not wrap my brain around those words, as hard as I tried. They were not my own truth, and so they became foreign. She might as well have been speaking to me in Swahili. That's how incomprehensible they were to me.

A few nights before, we'd been eating sushi in Toledo.

"There's a new restaurant we need to try," she'd texted me that morning. "I'll pick you up at 6:00."

"Yay! I'll be ready," I texted back.

Then I proceeded to rearrange my entire life so I could eat sushi with her. It had become the norm. I didn't tell her no, didn't want to tell her no.

We were bellied up to the sushi bar, enjoying spicy tuna rolls, and the restaurant was packed. We shared a bottle of wine, then ordered a second. As we talked about her latest love interest on Tinder, Cecilia began slurring her words.

"Here's the thing, Katrina," she said, "I'm always going to date boys. I like them. I can't create a forever kind of life with you because I'm not gay."

"I don't understand," I said, my face warm with Cabernet, my inhibitions unleashed. "It seemed like you were pretty gay when my tongue was on your pussy." I giggled then, my vulgar, unexpected comeback making me brave and giddy.

I noticed the couple next to us turn their heads in shock. I didn't care. How in the world could she say she wasn't gay—or at least bi—when we'd had sex multiple times? When she'd been the one to initiate it?

"Jesus Fucking Christ," she said, her voice getting louder. "What do I have to say to get it through your head?"

She stood up, wobbly, and headed toward the door. As she grabbed the handle, she turned to face me. With all the drama she could muster, she yelled, "I'm not like you, Katrina! I'm not fucking gay!"

And then she left me, red-cheeked and mortified at the counter, my giddiness stomped into the ground under the square heel of her Versace boots. I kept my back to the rest of the customers, but I could hear their hushed voices and stifled laughter as my face burned a hole in the night. The quiet that came over the entire place suffocated me. She left me with the bill, and I didn't even know if I had enough money in my account to cover it. I walked out of the restaurant with my head down, trying not to cry in front of a room full of strangers. Then I realized she'd taken the car and left me in Toledo. I Ubered home, embarrassed and broken and still so very in love with her.

In *The Fisher King and the Handless Maiden*, Robert Fisher writes that Sanskrit has ninety-six words for love, ancient Persian has eight, Greek has three, and English has only one. He surmises that the reason we have only one word for love is because we don't give that realm of feeling enough importance. Conversely, Eskimos have thirty words for snow because it is so vital to have exact information about the element that could provide them either life or death.

Ninety-six words for *love.* Love for significant others. Love for friends. Love for sexual partners. Love for children. Love for ideology. Love for animals. Love for the land. For food. For air. For the salty sea. For the wind in our hair. So many kinds of love. So much love.

But the ones that describe that essential human relationship—be it man/woman, man/man, woman/woman, or any other genders—those become blurry for me. And not indistinguishably blurry. I have female friends I'm not one bit attracted to physically. But when all those attractions converge? When spirituality, intellect, and skin collide, how do you distinguish *in love* from *love*?

She loved me. That she freely admitted. But *in love?*

She could not go there.

And I was left reeling from that rejection, that gut punch.

She had always asserted her heterosexuality. I am the first woman she'd ever been physically intimate with. I understood that it was scary, unnerving, outside the norm. I chose an easy life with an adoring husband and four beautiful kids when I could have just as easily run off into the mountains with the girl of my dreams. But the former was easier, more acceptable. That didn't mean it was less, it just was—exactly what it was. Society imposed certain restrictions on us, and I readily embraced and accepted them for twenty-eight years.

But I had tasted her.

She had tasted me.

We had wrapped ourselves up in miles and conversation and sheets and sweat.

There was no going back.

And so, that *I'm not in love with you. Someday, I might want to be with another man* became a wound, deep and raw.

The notion that she might choose a yet-to-be-discovered human over an I-love-you-more-than-life companion who stood beside her through tears and laughter and fights and *fuck yous* felt like the ultimate abandonment.

Was it me?

Was it society?

Was it her?

Was it anatomy?

How did that all get unraveled into truths and revelations?

"Can you not just rest easy in the love she's able to provide?" Allison asked. "Can you not just be happy there?"

But I couldn't.

She could fuck as many men as she wanted to fuck.

But to say *I'm not in love with you* ripped my heart into a million little paper pieces, to be scattered throughout the universe, riding hot winds and landing in city gutters and mountain grasses, all the places we'd shared side by side, all those we had yet to explore.

"What we have together is in many ways so much more than I've had with anyone, including any man," she'd said.

And I wondered, then *why*?

Why not say, "You. You. You. There's no one like you."

Because for me, there was no one like her.

No one.

Not in forty-six years.

I would have left it all behind for her.

Had already left so much of it behind for her.

I didn't want to be left behind by her.

* * *

Dear Cecilia,

Here's where I am today.

I think I'm going to stay with him.

Maybe I'll even move out of the guest room, little by little. I'll start with a couple pairs of shoes. Some pajamas. A hat, a book, a purse, a brush, my laundry basket. Maybe later, my body. Perhaps someday, my soul.

But probably not.

It is already irrevocably tangled up in you.

I began this letter as I peered at my computer through late-night tears, trying to wrangle all my strongest emotions into words that would move her, words that might possibly make her consider staying in my life.

There is much about him to love, after all—his laugh, his big heart, his blue eyes, his commitment to our kids, his culinary skills, that thick silver mane. Maybe I can fall madly in love with him, given time and attention. If not, maybe his love for me can sustain us both. A million times a day, he says he loves me. He has so much love, and I have so little. But he has always, above all, been my good and faithful friend.

And I'd rather eat my own pain than cause someone else's. I suppose that's the Pisces in me.

I'm not sure I even believe in love anymore with its inequity and quicksand and treachery.

It breaks me in two to hear you proclaim your love and longing for your Russian lover, to have you cancel plans with me not because of him but because of the memory of him. It's hard to hear about the someday relationships you might want to have. The yet unknowns. The to-be-discovereds. It levels me ... because I stand in front of you day after day after day saying, Here I am. I will not hurt you. I will not leave you. I will hold you carefully when you need a safe space and release you gently when you need to fly. As long as you fly back to me. Create something with me. Me. Me. Me.

But I am not what you want or need.

And I don't want you to stop talking, to stop sharing those intimate pieces of you, no matter how sharp the edges.

That must be just how Charles feels.

With a sharp-edged knife in my heart, I considered how my husband of so many years might feel about my relationship with this woman with whom I'd become obsessed. Didn't he deserve more? More compassion? More consideration? More love than I felt for her?

If I stay with him, he'll be happy again. And I'll get some of the things my own heart needs ... a hand to grasp on the street, fingers intertwined, someone to hold at night, to wake with in the morning, to share coffee and contemplation, to kiss by the fire. When he wraps his arms around me, I'll close my eyes from time to time—maybe too much, too often ... maybe every time—and imagine it's you instead. I'll feel the memory of your hair on my cheek. I'll recall the curve of your spine as you sleep. His lips don't feel like yours—they are sandpaper and bourbon in comparison to your dark wine and cashmere—but I'll remember.

I'll always remember.

That will have to be enough.

Maybe he and I will get that little house on St. George Island that we've always talked about. Maybe you'll come visit. But never as often as I'd like. Maybe you'll have your own room, and I'll slip into bed beside you at night, just to hear you breathe. Maybe you'll hold my hand on a cool, starry night as we stare into the vast ocean black together, toes in the water, salt on our faces. Maybe you'll kiss me there, in the dark, under a moon that illuminates everything so much bigger than us, in a space that doesn't care about how our corporeal selves were formed, only about who we are when we're together. Maybe I'll just dream about that night instead. Again and again and again. Maybe some nights, the house will be ours, yours and mine.

Our astrological counselor—the one you introduced me to—says you are as connected to me as you were to your Russian, but that you aren't ready to accept what that means, what that kind of future might look like, what kind of work and acceptance and risk that might take. That you wake up some mornings afraid and ashamed of what you feel for me, that unconventional, unexpected same love. That other mornings, you wake missing and wanting me.

The second mornings—those are the ones I'll think about.

Because I can't change who I am.

A woman.

A friend.

A once-lover.

I can't make you feel what you don't.

I would never ask that of you.

And I also can't compartmentalize you—to put you in a box that says best friend and nothing more. That would be false, and I will not give you false. I cannot live in half-truths. I will always give you every bit of what I feel with honesty and vulnerability. I'm not even sure I'm capable of anything less. I would be outed as a fraud immediately. Because you are in me and around me and all over me. You are my skin and my breath and my heart. So I will learn to live with all my nerves exposed to the elements because I cannot learn to live without you.

I don't want to learn. I never want those synapses to fire.

Friend. Lover. Companion. Partner.

I'll take whatever you are able to give. No more, no less.

The memory of Cecilia's Russian lover finding and reading the letters I'd written—then screaming accusations at her, about us—surfaced painfully in my mind.

Yes, your Russian lover was right when he read the letters I'd written you, professing my love. Yes, I love you as you love him. Yes, Charles loves me as I love you. None of it is simple or equal or easily navigable.

Fuck love with all its inconsistency and heartbreak and pain.

Fuck love that cannot be returned.

Fuck the unrequited.

Fuck it all, disassemble it, and then gather the salvageable parts back up into my shaking hands. That's what I plan to do. Those are the pieces I'll choose to hold onto ... the good, the true, the undeniable, the golden, the ones with the soft edges and the laughter. The rest, I'll let go of. I'll try not to look back. Sometimes, though, I know I will. There is still a longing in me. An ache. A tangle of what ifs and whys and why nots. Eventually, it will subside.

All pain does.

Mend your own broken, love. For however long it takes. I

will stand with and beside you through it … up close or at a distance. In whatever capacity you need. We'll laugh and talk and travel and wine and dine and hold each other carefully … wherever and however it feels best. Safe. Happy. Content.

Today, I plan to stay with him.

Tonight, I might change my mind.

Tomorrow, if you asked me to leave him, you know what I would do.

Love,

Katrina

CHAPTER 9

The cockpit was warm and stuffy. My seat by the window, a view into the vastness of the darkening sky. I was flying to Colorado alone. Cecilia and I had planned this trip for months, had eagerly anticipated two days in Boulder, three in Aspen. She texted me pictures of the Airbnb she'd rented in the mountains. *Isn't it the cutest?* And it was. It was perfect. A writing retreat for me while she went to the Pilates studio. Evenings free for dinner and wine together. For us. Just us.

Then four days before our departure, she sent the email. The one that said she needed to distance herself. That I was toxic for her. That she was not in love with me.

The one that split me in two.

In the midst of tears and angst and uncertainty, I thought about changing my ticket, about flying somewhere different, somewhere new, somewhere that didn't feel like an open wound. I'd considered Manhattan briefly because in a strange and quirky twist, I'd met a woman online named Lily when I had been with Cecilia in New York. Cecilia and I had been on Tinder for kicks—she was looking for boys, me for girls. I'd seen Lily's picture on my phone and had been immediately taken aback. She was head-turningly gorgeous with her snow white hair and her ocean eyes. Her smile was contagious. I'd flipped quickly through her photos—pensive, fun, quirky. I'd read her brief description—insightful, funny, endearing—and I'd immediately swiped right without a second thought, wanting to somehow make an unlikely connection.

A partial list of her "favorites" seared itself into my memory: *my nieces, kitchen dancing, freshly shaved legs on clean, white sheets.*

We matched, and I felt a little jolt of electricity.

I'm getting ready to get on the subway, so I'm going to lose you soon, she messaged.

I'm getting ready to fly back to Ohio, I replied.

Ohio? she messaged back. *That seems like a long way away.*

Not too far to fly, I replied.

I'm jumping on the Subway to meet a friend. About to lose service, she said.

A friend? A girlfriend? A date?

I didn't want her to lose me, so I gave her my phone number.

She and I had been communicating via text and phone for months after that initial exchange. I'd run outside to take her calls so I could talk to her privately without my kids hearing. I'd laugh at her silly jokes and puns and blush when she'd tell me how pretty my eyes were. She'd read my recently published novel and was the one person I trusted with the first draft of my memoir. I'd fed it to her as I wrote it, chapter by chapter, with feelings of both excitement and trepidation. She always responded with high praise and admiration.

I love it, she'd text. *You're an amazing writer.*

There was something about her. Something true and substantial. Something loving and safe. Something that kept me coming back, even when I wasn't sure where I was going. I'd looked at every one of her pictures online. Had marveled at the warmth of her smile, the devotion of her friends and family. She exuded kindness and familiarity and fun.

But my heart was still tangled up in Cecilia, this Colorado trip was paid for, my seat on the plane secure, and Charles had already rearranged his schedule to cover the kids. Colorado was one of the places Cecilia and I had shared together. It seemed I might need to heal here. To write through the pain. To finish the story in the shadow of the Flatirons.

Our story had begun so innocuously. Four tickets to see Taylor Swift, gifted by Allison because she couldn't manage the trip to Detroit in the middle of a work emergency. So I'd told Marley to invite two friends, but she only wanted to bring one—Cecilia's daughter, Chloe. Cecilia gave her own tickets away, and the four of us went together, mothers and daughters. A small road trip and a lifelong memory.

The only song I'd really known before the concert was "Shake It Off," but the girls screamed every word to every song while they cried happy tears. As I watched Taylor perform, her song lyrics leached into my soul and became a part of me. Somehow, I knew "Clean," with its simple beauty and transcendent metaphor of rain, would eventually mean so much more to me. But I had no idea then that the cleansing I'd need would be from my all-encompassing obsession with Cecilia.

We drank overpriced beers and reveled in our girls' enthusiasm and excitement as we were introduced to Vance Joy and Shawn Mendes. When Taylor took the stage, she shimmied in pink sequins, made elaborate costume changes, sang a duet with Imagine Dragons, and strutted down the makeshift runway with Martha Hunt and Gigi Hadid. We were all entranced. Cecilia and I were drunk, not from beer, but from fun and laughter and the beauty of watching our kids' pure happiness.

After the concert, we all ran to our hotel in a driving rain, splashing and laughing and singing to the slick streets. The girls whispered and giggled themselves to sleep in their adjoining room as Cecilia and I shared the farthest edges of a king-sized bed. It was an unexpectedly fun night, an evening to water the seeds of a blossoming friendship. As the new girl in our small town, I was so grateful to have met Cecilia.

The next morning, as we were loading up her Range Rover and my back was aching from the previous night's dancing, she said, "I can fix that, you know." And I scheduled my first private Pilates class while she whispered on the phone to her mysterious Russian lover.

* * *

When my plane landed in Denver and I stepped into the familiar airport, my breath caught in my throat. *I can't do this*, I thought. *I can't be here. Not alone. Not without her.* When my Uber drove past the Omni where we used to stay together, I felt the cold, hard fist in my chest. Then Boulder, the Pearl Street Mall. It was late, dark, and no one could see my tears. But they overtook and owned me. I cried myself to sleep in my rented Airbnb bed, clutched my pillow like a life raft, tried not to think about the sound of her breath beside me. About her slapping my hands off her back in our shared bed and growling, "Get your hot hands off of me."

About the void, the emptiness, the space she created by request. The rejection. The abandonment.

The next morning, I sat at Trident, sipping coffee and trying to write my way out of melancholy when "Cherry Bomb" began playing over the cafe speakers. It was the soundtrack of the Joan Jett and Cherie Curry story, the one we'd watched in Grand Haven. I heard Cecilia's off-key voice singing the lyrics, explaining the complicated musical history, saw her waving her long, lean arms in the air. When she danced to rock music, I always thought of her on stage, in pointe shoes, her gorgeous body creating magic and art. If I have any regrets in this life, it's that I never had the opportunity to see her dance ballet. I imagine she was the purest grace and beauty. I see it in her fingertips, in her stride, in the lift of her chin. I think about her in a leotard, strong and sensual and focused and leonine—ready to pounce or protect, depending on who you were in her world.

And thinking about all of this, all of her past, present, and future, I felt myself crumbling. Decomposing. Turning into fragments of bone and ash.

I felt the sting of being so easily discarded burning a hole in my chest.

I texted Charles.

We were still trying to come to terms with ourselves and with each other. We were in the full disclosure/brutal honesty stage, and it felt right to share my feelings with him.

It is so beautiful here, and I am so empty and sad. What is wrong with me?

He texted back immediately.

You are loved and lovely. You control your story. Tell me five things that are wonderful about you.

That's too many, I replied. Five too many.

You are not a deficit, he said. Your story is an addition. People (including me) love you. Why is that? You need to speak those reasons. There are millions of them, but I want just five.

Nothing seems true anymore, I said. If I say I'm kind, it's not true ... because I've been unkind to you. Same for loyal and empathetic and loving and and and ...

Perfect is not possible. We are not capable of not having bumps or stumbles. So, five things. For real. Five things.

I could not answer for a long time. Everything seemed contrived. Finally, I sent these:

Kind

Fun

Loving

Good friend

Good writer

Yes, he affirmed. This is you. This is who you are. This is the story that is yours. You are you. You are complete with these things. You are not made whole by others. You are already complete. You bring yourself to them and they choose to tag along with you or not. Those that choose not to don't take away from you. They just don't get to add to themselves. Now go sing your song around those five things. You can control your narrative and it can be what you want it to be. I love you. You add to me.

That achingly beautiful kindness, in the midst of all the pain we'd inflicted upon each other—a reminder of who I was and who he was.

Who we both once were.

Who we had—during some precious times—been together.

PART TWO:

THE EYEWALL

Hurricanes are dangerous and destructive. Known also as cyclones and typhoons in other parts of the world, hurricanes cause high winds, flooding, heavy rain, and storm surges.

Learn more about hurricanes and other tropical storms so you can be prepared to keep your family safe.

(SOURCE: cdc.gov)

CHAPTER 10

"How can I say I truly love you if I don't embrace and love all of you?" Charles said during a particularly intense and painful conversation. "I've always known on some level who you are. I made a commitment to you—to all of you. I will honor that. I will honor every bit of you. Even if it doesn't include me."

Owning my feelings for the woman I had fallen so desperately for, discussing them at length, examining them together under a microscope, created a new and interesting dynamic between my husband and me. In the conversations of our youth—when we were still so incredibly young and uncomfortable and unsure—he jokingly, obnoxiously said things to me such as: "If you're going to be with a woman, at least let me watch." And: "I think the most emasculating thing you can do is leave me for another woman." And: "Are you wearing your life partner sandals today?" when I chose the least feminine, most comfortable shoes I owned.

Nearly three decades ago, we were teenagers, young and in love. We swam naked in Brown County ponds on his weekend visits to Bloomington. We were idealistic and starry-eyed and wild with lust and big dreams. We had plans to put a basketball court in the basement of the mansion we'd someday build with our hard-earned millions. We gave life to and grew four lovely human beings. We laughed and cried and traveled and stayed home. We made money. We lost money. We fought vehemently about money. We built and sold houses, we moved to different states. We changed our views on religion and politics—not necessarily in tandem. And we supported and loved each other through it all, no judgment, no ultimatums. At least not out loud.

"You are all I need in this life," Charles said to me again and again.

But he was not all I needed. I was fed by too many. It's a fundamental difference between the two of us. He had, for so many years, been my alpha. But I have had deep friendships, more expansive and complicated needs.

"My island is small," he said. "And I want to choose who gets to be on it." I understood that about him. Just as he understood that my island was party central, that nearly everyone got an invitation, that I most always wanted to be surrounded by the laughter of friends and family.

But during the times I was with Cecilia, he was notably sad. I felt guilty for spending so much time away, selfish for wanting so much for myself.

Charles and I decided to have sex because it had been such a long time since we'd connected physically. I'd moved into the guest room weeks before, and we were living much more as roommates than lovers. Our conversations consisted primarily of surface details. *Are you going to the grocery store? Who's taking Jack to orchestra rehearsal? How much money is left in our joint account? Have you heard from Scott?*

We texted about it first. *Should we? Do you want to? Will it help? Will it hurt? Will it provide clarity? Or more confusion?*

And ultimately, he texted, *Please. I miss you.*

I was nervous. Apprehensive. This man I'd been intimate with a million times before. The father of my four children. It scared me, this encounter. Mostly because I didn't know how I'd feel, especially after being with Cecilia. I was afraid to feel nothing, I think. Nothing is always worse than sad or angry or upset.

My mom used to say about my dad, "When you reach the point of indifference, then you'll know you're finished."

That night with Charles felt different.

It was so many of my greatest fears realized.

The void that had been growing deep and wide inside of me swallowed me whole. I closed my eyes in the dark so I wouldn't see it; focused my mind on other things so I wouldn't think about it. But it was there, gnawing, gnawing, making itself known regardless.

He and I had always held different thoughts about sex. I believe you can have sex that's just sex. Maybe that's because I've been forced to have sex that I didn't want; that I was taught early in life that sex was a transaction, not an emotional bond. He feels differently. Sex, for him, is always connected. Always.

But that night.

My body was there, and my heart was not.

The room was dark, and my feet were cold. I longed for a pair of warm socks. We'd left our yellow lab, Lucy, outside the bedroom, and she pawed at the door, whining to be let back in. I looked out the window at our backyard pool, at the shimmering pond beyond. I wondered if the dogs had already been fed. Those were the things I noticed, thought about, and experienced.

It felt like a nail in the coffin of our marriage.

It felt like some kind of gut-wrenching finale. The tragic, star-crossed deaths of Romeo and Juliet.

It felt like I was already gone.

"It's been hard having you gone so much," Charles said after. "When you were spending so much time with Cecilia, I was lonely."

I tried not to think about how that might feel to him because I was weak and selfish, and I didn't have the capacity to hold his pain along with my own. I tried not to imagine him in his oversized leather chair at night, reading dissertations and sipping bourbon while my floral recliner sat empty and unused, my wine glass clean and put away in the cupboard, waiting for the day when our lives might return to the normal and expected. When we might sit again in silence, side by side, in our own private worlds.

We discussed many ways to try to balance our relationship equation, to try to save our marriage. We discussed it with our counselor, Laurel; we talked about it with our closest friends. He had, of course, told me to find a girlfriend, but it wasn't easy when I did. It was far from easy. When I was with Cecilia, he was understandably lonely. And inside that loneliness was where all the fear and questioning and insecurity made its home.

"I wish you'd plan a boys' weekend," I said. "Reconnect with your old friends, go out for drinks, chase women, listen to music. It would be so good for you."

But he stayed home.

"I wish you'd make some new friends here in Ohio," I said. "Most of your friends are in Indiana and Mississippi, and proximity matters. It would be nice for you to have a drinking buddy, someone to play golf or bike with. Why don't you go find that person? Join a golf league or a biking group?"

But he didn't.

And when those ideas fizzled out, I said. "Do you want to date? Would that make you feel less lonely?"

His response, my greatest fear, realized: "Yes."

It made me queasy to imagine him alone with another woman, to think about his hands on the small of her back. It was hypocritical for me to feel that way, but in this one way, it wasn't: He would always be the only man I ever loved. There would never be another beyond him. It was either going to be him forever for me, or it was going to be a woman. The thought of him with another woman felt redundant to me. It felt like a replacement. One soft body for another. A head full of long hair exchanged for a head full of, perhaps, another color. Intertwined fingers that felt a little different, but mostly the same. Soft and supple from lotions and potions. Smooth from waxing. The scents, familiar.

We have friends in an open marriage and asked them all the pertinent questions. *How did it work? How did you keep your relationship primary? How did you establish rules and boundaries? How did it feel? How might it fail?*

"It's a beautiful thing to see the one you love happy and fulfilled," Christine told me. "It's a concept called compersion. When Steve comes home and tells me all about his dates, it fills me. I know without a doubt that I will always be his number one, and I love to see him so happy. Opening our marriage has expanded our relationship, it doesn't detract from it."

I wanted to see Charles happy. I wanted to see if our relationship could be expanded when all I'd done recently was detract from it.

"But what about jealousy?" I asked.

"I don't feel any jealousy," Christine said. "It's all about establishing rules and boundaries and sticking to them. That way, there are no surprises and no secrets."

Charles and I read books, we consulted websites, we tried to create a safe space, we established our rules of engagement. The most important of them: full disclosure, no lies, no omissions.

We created accounts on multiple dating sites, including Tinder, OKCupid, and Plenty of Fish. Our accounts specified that we were a married couple looking to extend our sexual experiences. Then we created individual accounts that said, *In an open marriage.* We both set our gender preferences to women.

I vacillated between fear and excitement. Everything in my Catholic bones was screaming, *Stop! Don't do it!* I'd been taught that sex was wrong if it wasn't for procreation within a marriage, and I'd carried the weight of those guilty pleasures with me throughout my life. My confused moral compass was spinning wildly.

But it was fun to choose our pictures together, to help Charles write his profile. In those moments, we felt connected again.

"What should I say my hobbies are?" he asked.

"Definitely cooking," I said. "Maybe entertaining? You're great at hosting a party."

"You should probably not include cooking in yours," he laughed. "But definitely include that you're a writer. That's sexy."

"Well, everyone will see by my pictures that I'm sexy," I joked.

"That's my girl," he said. "I like it when you see yourself the way I see you."

But I didn't really see myself the way Charles did. Writing about myself in a sexual way was uncomfortable and more than a little bit scary. Knowing what we were soliciting made my stomach churn. I wondered if I would be able to be in a threesome with someone else. To actually watch Charles be intimate with another. I didn't really enjoy heterosexual sex to begin with. Now we were bringing a second woman in?

We quickly learned that what we were looking for—a woman who wanted to be in a sexual relationship with a married couple—was called a unicorn. Rare and difficult to find, unicorns in the dating world were few and far between. Most women wanted to either be with me or to be with Charles, not with both of us.

We decided that we'd try our luck individually, and if we liked the person we met, we'd discuss the prospect of a threesome.

Charles's heterosexual prospects in our small, conservative Ohio town were much more expansive than mine, and he immediately matched with a woman named Vivian. The night they went out on a date together, I was sick with fear and discomfort and jealousy. I could not wrap my head around the notion that my husband was on a date with another woman. Yes, we had agreed to it. But living it was something else altogether. The minutes ticked by like hours as my mind imagined a million lust-filled scenarios. All four kids were out with their friends, so I was home alone, pacing. I called Christine multiple times so she could help talk me off the ledge.

When Charles came home, he approached our conversation gently.

"How much do you want to know?" he asked.

"All of it," I said. "Everything."

Christine and Steve had told us that they feel differently about disclosure. Steve wants to know every detail of Christine's dates, but Christine doesn't want to know anything about Steve's. I couldn't imagine not knowing. The not knowing would have made me crazy with speculation, the scenarios in my overactive imagination worse, probably, than any reality.

My hands were shaking as Charles began to tell me the story of their date.

"She was really kind," he said. "And smart. She's a little bit on the heavy side, but she's beautiful."

"Beautiful?" I asked, feeling the nausea stir within me.

"Yes. Striking," he said. "Long, curly hair. Huge dimples." And then sensing my discomfort he added, "But not as beautiful as you."

"What did you talk about?" I asked.

He began to tell me about her job, a foundation that she'd begun. Her three kids at home; the one she'd lost as a baby. But my brain couldn't focus on his words. All I could think about was the two of them, sitting together at a table, heads bent toward each other, sharing personal pieces of themselves.

"Did you hold hands?" I asked.

"Yes."

"Did you kiss her?"

"Yes."

"In your car?" I asked.

"At the bar," he said.

"You made out at a bar?" I asked.

"Yes. But I wouldn't call it 'making out.' It was a kiss."

"With tongue?" I asked.

"Katrina, stop," he said. "It was just a kiss."

But my mind was stuck on that kiss, on that intimacy, on his lips meeting hers. On his lips meeting anyone else's.

"But here's the best part," Charles said. "She wants to meet you."

I didn't know what to say. My mind was racing. This woman who had spent the evening with—and kissed—my husband wanted to meet me, too. Was I ready for this? Did I want this? Were we really considering doing this?

"There's a craft beer festival in her hometown Saturday night," he said. "She wants us to meet her there. It's a little over an hour away."

The first thing I thought about was our kids, sitting home on a Saturday night, texting friends or watching a movie while their parents hooked up with another woman. *What in the world were we thinking? What kind of parents did that? Even if their kids were all self-sufficient teenagers?* But we had agreed to this together. It wasn't fair for me to back out now.

"Okay," I said. "Let's meet her."

That's how we found ourselves wandering through a small Michigan town on a Saturday afternoon listening to a decent live band playing John Mellencamp and drinking craft beer. The day was unseasonably cool for late summer, and the leaves were just beginning to show signs of how beautifully red and yellow they were about to become.

The season of change was imminent.

"There she is," Charles said, standing up to greet Vivian.

They hugged as I stood awkwardly behind Charles.

"Vivian," he said, "this is my wife, Katrina."

"It's so great to meet you!" Vivian said, hugging me warmly and unexpectedly.

"It's so good to meet you, too," I said. "Charles has told me so much about you."

"Well, don't believe everything he says," she said with an unearned sense of familiarity.

Was this woman telling me not to believe my own husband of twenty-two years? This woman who spent one evening with him? My hackles were up, and I smiled stiffly.

"Let's get you a beer," Charles said.

"Yes, please!" Vivian said.

"I'll wait here and save our seats," I said as I watched them walk away, talking and laughing together. At one point, he put his hand on the small of her back, and I felt a sense of panic blooming in my stomach.

But as the day stretched into night and numerous beers were consumed, I began to loosen up a bit, to share in their banter, to laugh at their jokes. Vivian really was as smart and interesting as Charles had reported, and I was mesmerized by her dimples.

When the band announced their final number, Vivian invited us to her place for another drink.

Charles looked at me with anticipation and excitement, and I nodded to let him know I was willing to move forward.

Vivian's studio apartment was cute and cozy with eclectic decor and lots of tchotchkes from her extensive travels. There were pictures of her kids in every available space, their bright eyes shining with happiness. Charles and I sat down on her orange couch while she made us Manhattans in her tiny kitchen.

"I hope you'll forgive the mess," she said. "I asked my kids to clean the place up before they went to their dad's, but teenage cleaning standards are very different from Mom cleaning standards."

"Don't we know it!" Charles laughed. "I don't understand why it's so hard for them to carry their shoes from the living room to their bedroom. Or to rinse out their cereal bowls. It just boggles my mind."

Vivian handed Charles his drink, set mine on the table in front of me, and sat down next to me.

"May I kiss you?" she asked.

I was taken aback by her immediate and brazen approach, and my body tingled with a mixture of fear, apprehension, and excitement.

When her lips met mine, I thought about Cecilia. The softness, the gentleness—it felt so familiar. I closed my eyes and lost myself in the memory of her until Charles stepped in and began to kiss Vivian.

I sat back on the couch, unsure about what to do next.

Charles took each of our hands in his and said, "Let's go to bed."

I enjoyed kissing Vivian, but I was too distracted by all the arms and legs jockeying for position in her queen sized bed to really immerse myself in the experience. I felt out of place and uncomfortable as I watched Charles kiss another woman, and I didn't know how to assert myself into their togetherness. Although the beer and bourbon fog helped ease some of the discomfort of being in bed with my husband and a virtual stranger, I could not get past the sight of my husband touching and kissing another woman, his hands exploring her most intimate places. When he came inside of her and collapsed on her heaving chest, I felt cold and alone and a world away, even though we were only separated by a rumpled, down-filled comforter.

* * *

"It's just not my thing," I said to Charles when we discussed the possibility of another threesome.

"So it's over?" he asked. "Just like that? What about our agreement?"

"We agreed to try," I said. "And I did that. I just don't want to do it again."

"What about dating others?" he asked. "Are we going to keep doing that?"

"Well, you're really the only one dating right now." I was still texting Lily in New York, but we hadn't yet met in person.

Charles communicated with lots of women online. Occasionally, he went on dates alone. One night, he didn't come home at all. It was all confusing and hurtful. I was spinning, breaking, questioning. I wanted to take everything back, to close our marriage again, but it was too late. There was no returning to what and who we were before.

We decided to go back to counseling to try and work through our latest mistakes.

In Laurel's office, we sat in separate chairs, hands clasped in our laps, brown walls and matching throw pillows creating a soft, cozy space.

But nothing about being there felt safe to me.

Laurel asked hard questions, and we struggled for answers. When something I said hit home, I could feel Charles tense, could see out of the corner of my eye the defensive smirk he donned. Then the shifting of legs, the heavy, loud sigh. And I knew he was ready to fire back.

We were both so many people during those days, each of us alternately filled with love and longing and then anger and jealousy. We took turns talking of not being heard, of not being seen, of abandonment and sadness. We avoided each other one day and missed each other the next.

"It's hard," I admitted, "to watch him jump so easily into other women's beds. I mean, I'm trying to figure out my own sexuality, and he just wants to have lots of sex with different women. It makes me feel replaced. He's the only man I'll ever love, but if we separate, he'll easily replace me with another woman. In fact, when we were with another woman, it felt like he already had."

"What makes you feel like Charles is more interested in other women than he is in you?" Laurel asked.

"Because during our threesome, all his attention was on the other woman. He barely even noticed I was there."

"That's because you and I already have a connection," he said in defense. "I wanted to make sure our third didn't feel left out."

"You're so chivalrous" I said, my voice heavy with sarcasm. "I think it's pretty hard for someone to feel left out when you choose to come inside her and only her."

"Oh, is that it?" he asked. "Now we're going to talk about who I have an orgasm with?"

"Well, it's no longer with me," I said. "That feels like something important to discuss."

That's how it went between us—from kind, loving words to angry accusations. From building each other up to tearing each other apart. We understood each other one moment, and we were complete strangers the next. We were both on a roller-coaster, careening into the unknown. I knew he was scared and hurt and unsettled. I was, too. Our lives were out of control, reckless. We were sleeping with other people to determine whether we should stay together. Nothing about it made any sense at all.

We sifted through the past five years of change and realignment and separation. We tried to pinpoint when it all began to fall apart.

Was it in Zanesville when his job changed? Was it the uprooting in Mississippi? Did we lose each other in the swampy heat and Southern accents? Was it Ohio, when we tried to rebuild something that had—for too many years—been irreparably cracking?

I thought about the Memorial and Labor Day weekends that we shared in Ohio with our closest Indiana and Ohio friends. The Hoosiers would make the pilgrimage for the long weekend, and we'd drink through the next seventy-two hours. Ten adults and seventeen kids, give or take a few. The kids would set up tents in the backyard, and they'd have diving contests in the pool. We'd swim in the pond with our beer koozies and our pool noodles. I'd count heads over and over again, making sure all the kids were accounted for. We'd find them in trees, in tents, in the kitchen. They ate every ounce of guacamole we made, and then they ran their fingers across the bottom of the bowl to get the remnants.

The last Labor Day weekend we hosted, we'd invited Cecilia to join us. She arrived in an Uber, already a little drunk. She was loud and possessive with me. I could tell my friends felt uncomfortable with her, but I continued to drink away that truth. She asked me to go with her to deliver something to her ex-husband, and I didn't hesitate. I climbed into an Uber, leaving my husband, my kids, and my invited friends at my home. We were gone far longer than I'd anticipated, and as I began to sober up, I thought: *What am I doing? Who leaves her own party? Who abandons her friends who drove three hours to see her?* In the days of Cecilia, I became someone I didn't recognize, someone my family didn't recognize, someone my friends didn't want to recognize. Then Charles and I opened up our marriage, and he began to do the same. We made so many bad decisions; decisions we never would have made before.

The bottom line was this: We were losing ourselves. We were losing each other.

"I enjoy working with you two," Laurel told us. "You're very adept at examining yourselves and each other deeply. Most of the time it's just head-butting and fighting and argument after argument. And Katrina, I'm still impressed with how supportive Charles has been about your sexual exploration."

Immediately, I stiffened and became defensive. Yes, he supported my initial exploration, but now I was supporting his, too. And before I questioned my sexuality, he'd never hinted that he wanted to sleep with other women. I was not about to let Charles be the hero in this story. This story had way too many layers.

I repeated all the things I'd done for him over the years, reminded her of all the ways I'd supported his education and his career, talked about what I'd sacrificed in order to make his dreams come to fruition.

"Yes. I understand," Laurel said. "But ultimately, he gave you the green light to have an affair."

I squirmed in my seat, felt the heat reddening my cheeks.

An affair? That's the word it all boils down to? Was it an affair if he gave me permission? If we talked about it openly and honestly? What about the woman we'd both slept with? The women he'd slept with alone? Was that an affair on his part, too? Why was his willingness to let me explore my sexuality more important than all the sacrifices I'd made for him and for our family? Why was his permission-giving the weight that tipped the scales in his favor? And why did he have to give me permission in the first place? Wasn't that decision mine to be made? Was it because self-sacrifice is societally expected of a wife and mother? Because fidelity is, too? Because questions of identity and sexuality are too taboo to discuss in polite societal circles?

I understood in that single moment that I was perceived as the bigger villain, the bad guy, the one society and cultural norms wouldn't accept, the one who stepped a little too far outside the box. I understood, too, that if we could not save our marriage, I would always carry its demise on my shoulders alone—at least in the eyes of those who chose to see it that way.

And I ultimately found out there were so many who chose to see it that way.

The existing connection between Charles and I was tenuous at best, and the rejection of those open-marriage days was painful.

We began giving up on each other.

We began giving each other up.

The end of a relationship is never entirely one-sided. I don't know which of my transgressions broke him, but I know they were there. Festering. Aching.

Charles leaned into trying to save us as I leaned away.

"Please don't leave me," he said, as I peered over the edge of the abyss into the *what next.* "You are my everything."

But when someone you thought you knew turns out to be someone different, there's really no way to go back. At least there wasn't a way back for me.

"Then let's not go back," he said. "Let's go forward."

But I didn't know if my forward included him.

I didn't know anything.

Except how things get irrevocably twisted and damaged.

That, I was beginning to understand.

Twenty-eight years of history doesn't get broken in one fell swoop. In one action. In one reaction. It gets lost in the details. In the unsaids and the unacknowledgeds. It gets tangled up in the *"You said ..." "No, you said ..."* and the yelling and the crying and the pleading and the door slamming. It gets lost in the deepest hours of the night when you remember holding your babies and laughing and singing and dancing in the kitchen. When you recall him taking your chunky firstborn from your arms after a 2:00 AM feeding and saying, "Go rest. I've got him." And you wonder how those moments became another lifetime, a different existence. You don't even recognize who you once believed yourself to be.

And all your babies are taller than you now.

The break itself starts with a small fissure, a crack, hardly noticeable. You try to repair it so no one sees, but the glue doesn't hold. It's the wrong kind. You picked rubber cement instead of super glue. It seemed like a good idea at the time. You thought it would work. But you were wrong, and now it's too late. The crack has expanded. And now there are other cracks—some you created, some you didn't. But at this point, it doesn't matter. The cracks are splitting you both in two, and there is nothing you can do to fix them. So, you have to choose: break wide open and figure out how to stay in unrecognizable pieces and build something together from scratch. Or break away and take your pieces somewhere else to start again in a new and different form.

To redefine.

To enter into the next chapter with grace and dignity and honor.

To say, this season is over. And to accept that realization quietly and graciously. To grab your sweaters and boots and march into the next one, wind at your back, sun in your face, drying yesterday's tears as you go.

CHAPTER 11

"I'd like to ask you a favor," Charles said on an ordinary Friday morning while the kids were getting ready for school. Marley was blasting Halsey from her bedroom, and Jack was practicing his violin. It was a cacophony of happy sounds.

"What is it?" I replied, half-listening as I worked in my home office on an approaching deadline.

"One of Jess's boys is sick. We were supposed to meet at her house today, but we can't now. I'd like to bring her here. Would you mind working in a coffee shop this morning?"

Charles and Jess had been seeing each other for a couple of weeks. They'd met online, and she'd immediately become his primary focus. He'd shown me her dating profile picture, and her long, gray hair was striking. She lived locally and still had three kids at home—two things Charles had insisted he wasn't interested in when we began dating others.

"Why don't you meet *her* at a coffee shop?" I asked. "I'm working. Why do I have to pack up and go?"

And then it hit me. My anger was immediate and intense.

"You're bringing her here so you can fuck her, aren't you? You've had two coffee dates, and now it's time for the sex to commence? You're asking me to leave my own home—the place where I live and work and raise my children—so you can bring another woman here for a morning fuck, aren't you? You're bringing her into our co-parenting home, and you think that's okay?"

"Yes, Katrina," he said, his jawline setting, the anger in his voice rising to meet mine. "I've been very accommodating. I'd like this one favor from you. You spent ample time with Cecilia. This is the same thing."

"It's absolutely not the same thing," I said. "This is my home, our home, our children's home. This is where we live together, where we try to still have some semblance of normalcy for our family. Going to Jess's place is one thing. Having her come here? That's something else entirely."

A rage had been boiling under his surface for weeks now. Under mine, too. We had become increasingly short with each other. We had become enemies when we'd sworn to forever be friends. We were learning how to separate ourselves from each other, to lead individual lives while we raised our kids together, and we weren't doing it gracefully.

"She's willing to come into another woman's home to be fucked?" I asked, choosing profanity again and again to express the anger and devastation I was unable to articulate. "That's classy. She sounds like a keeper to me. By all means, bring her here. Fuck her. Just don't do it in my bed."

"I wouldn't think of it," he said angrily.

"I'll take the kids to school and leave for the day," I said. "Let me know when the fucking is done, and when it's safe to come home. And please take a shower. I'd prefer not to smell her on you."

"I'll be sure to do that." Jaws tense, square. Teeth gnashing.

I was angry with myself for agreeing to leave. Angrier with him for asking. Appalled at the thought of another woman agreeing to come into my home, with framed pictures of my kids on the walls, and fuck my husband—emotionally separated or not. I looked around at our wedding photos. Angrily,

I took them off the mantels, off the bookshelves, and shoved them all into a closet.

That Friday morning, I sat at the Flying Jed coffee shop while my husband had sex with another woman in my home. The home where my clothes hung in the closet, where my kids laid their heads at night, where my Hazelnut coffee creamer was in the refrigerator. I took a conference call, drank a cappuccino that burned all the way down, drafted an ebook about marketing agility. I texted Lily, tried to keep the conversation light and airy. I ordered my favorite cinnamon roll and choked down one bite. It tasted like sawdust and betrayal.

I wondered if Maggie and Lucy barked at Jess when she arrived, if they sat at the edge of the bed and watched. I wondered if Charles and Jess started kissing on my couch—the one where I wrapped myself in my favorite pink blanket and watched movies with my kids—before they moved to the spare bedroom, the one in which I'd carefully chosen the comforter, the sheets, the decorative pillows. Did he take her top off in the kitchen? Were they by the coffee pot where I poured my morning cup every day? Where he used to pour my cup for me every day? Did he pull her hair playfully as they were moving down the hallway? Did she notice the framed photos of me with my friends, with my sister, with my grand-niece, with my mom? Did either of them think of any of those things? Or was it just about the sweat and the moaning and the orgasm? Did he tell her how good she was, how satisfied she made him feel, in the same spaces where used to tell me the same things? Did he call her by name when he came inside her? Or did he slip and call her mine?

When I finally returned home that day, the air was different, stale, stagnant. Something that once lived there no longer did. Our former home became just a house. Four walls, some stairs, clothes in dressers, tools in the garage. Something died in the house that day. I thought about the wedding pictures shoved into the back of the closet and wondered if any of the glass had broken in my anger. I hoped it had. I hoped the jagged edges cut through my ivory wedding gown, tore into my perfectly coiffed hair, poked into my simultaneously hopeful and terrified twenty-four-year-old eyes.

We'd had such grand plans to be the best, most dedicated, most amicable co-parents. Those plans now seemed like the fantasies of a grade school child—learning to fly, becoming a horse, traveling to the moon. All seemed equally attainable now.

The following Saturday night—a mere twenty-four hours later—was Austin's senior fall play. Charles and I hadn't spoken.

"I'll drive separately," I said, not wanting to inhabit the same small space with Charles.

"Fine." His new passive-aggressive word of choice. "I'll meet you there," he said.

We sat in the same auditorium row, played the perfect parents, with Jack in between to create a living, breathing human buffer. We clapped for the actors and actresses, laughed when we were supposed to, smiled and nodded at fellow parents. We filed out into the lobby when the play was over and waited—in separate corners—for our boy.

And then I saw her.

I immediately began shaking. Her long, gray hair was unmistakable. I looked at him standing a few feet away from me in the lobby, trying to determine if he saw what I saw.

Did you know she was coming? I texted. *Did you invite her?*

She was flanked by her three young boys and her elderly parents. I watched them smile, interact, zip their coats. I watched Charles to see how he was reacting. My stomach churned.

I had no idea she'd be here, he texted back. *I swear to you.*

I'm going to the car, I texted, worried that I might vomit at any moment. *I don't believe you.*

I sat in the Navigator and tried to catch my breath. In, out. My reaction was visceral, animal.

You're so fucking full of shit, I texted from the car. *You knew she was going to be here. What the fuck are you trying to do? Are you trying to hurt me? Is this some kind of get-even game? This was our kid's senior play. What the fuck was she doing here?*

I swear to you, I didn't know she was coming, he texted back. *It's a total coincidence. I had no idea.*

A coincidence? You're a fucking liar, I texted. *Why the fuck would she just happen to bring her elementary school kids to a high school play where our son is performing the night after you fucked her IN OUR HOUSE?*

Fuck had become my go-to word of late. It conveyed all of my out-of-control rage and vitriol and anger and pain. I threw it at him relentlessly, used it as a verb, a noun, an adjective.

Katrina, you're being crazy, he texted back. *Stop. This is so ridiculous. I didn't know she was going to be here.*

Fucking liar.

Fucking liar.

Fucking liar.

For two excruciatingly long days, he maintained the charade. For two days he said things like: *Why would you think I'd do that to you? What do I have to gain? After twenty-eight years, do you not know me better? I can't believe you'd accuse me of lying. Do you know how hurtful that is? I thought you knew me better than that.* For forty-eight hours, he accused me of being hysterical and crazy, made me feel like I was losing my mind, like I was walking on quicksand, sinking, sinking. And I fully understood in the deepest parts of me that all that time, he was lying. My gut churned with that innate knowing, and for once, I listened.

Three nights after the play, he left his computer open to take a phone call on the deck, and I looked at his instant message history. I had never looked at his private texts before, had never invaded his space. Not in twenty-eight years. But I knew something was wrong. I knew it in my core. I thought I was going crazy. And there it was in black and white, the text from Saturday afternoon:

Hey, Pretty Lady. Kat's kinda uncomfortable with our transition right now, so it's probably best if we don't interact at the play tonight. I hope that doesn't bum you out. But I can't wait to see you again soon. And remember ... I'm a good student.

My stomach dropped. My knees gave. The lie. The sexual innuendo. I took a picture with my phone and showed it to him, hands shaking.

"Fuck you," I said.

His face went white.

"Fuck you for looking at my personal texts," he said, hot, red anger and defensiveness swirling through and out of him like a tornado.

"Fuck you for making me feel like I'm crazy," I said. "Fuck you for gaslighting me. Fuck you for lying straight to my face over and over. I'll admit that I shouldn't have looked at your text. But I think if you laid both our stories out on the table, my invasion of your private space would be forgiven before your manipulative, calculated lies. Fuck you. Fuck you. Fuck you."

And that was the evening everything shifted.

Forever.

CHAPTER 12

Charles had been on numerous dates since we opened our marriage. It seemed there were a million Midwestern women who were interested in a college professor with a shock of thick, white hair and cerulean eyes. There were substantially fewer women interested in a freelance writer and stay-at-home mom. I was no longer really interested in men, but in order to call this marriage over, I needed one more reassurance that I was, in fact, not straight. Not only was I curious, I was vengeful. I'd been so hurt by Charles and his lie about Jess that I wanted to strike back as hard as I could. So I decided to open my online dating options to men as well.

And that's when the matches flooded in.

I looked online for the most beautiful, attractive male I could find. When I swiped on Matthew, and we were declared a match by the Tinder powers that be, I felt a jolt of excitement and adventure. He was beautiful, muscular, and young. Young enough that I could have been his mother in another life.

He knew about Charles. Charles knew about him. There were no secrets, just sex.

It was my last ditch effort to understand this sinking ship, this opening, this invitation, this exploration.

When Matthew and I decided to meet at a bar in Michigan, I was perplexed by what to wear. Ripped jeans to indicate my desire to hold on to a bit of my youth? My square-heeled Stuart Weitzman pumps to convey that I was both elegant and financially established? I chose to combine them, to marry all the parts of me.

"My God, you're stunning," Matthew said when I entered the bar and chose the empty seat next to him. I knew him immediately from his Tinder pictures, his square jaw and his curly locks, gathered into a loose bun, tendrils of burnt gold on his thick neck. I had straightened my own unruly locks into a shining sheen of white blond, had applied a perfect coat of MAC Del Rio lipstick, had lined my eyes with a shade of almost-black. My mascara was thick and suggestive. I felt stunning. And bold.

I kissed him on the cheek as I sat and ordered a glass of Cabernet Sauvignon. He was drinking a Yuengling, our age difference apparent in our drinks of choice.

"Do you like wine?" I asked as I twirled the Cabernet in my glass.

"Not really," he said, with a bit of unnecessary apology in his voice. "I'm a beer guy through and through."

Matthew was shy and charming and a little bit nervous. We talked over drinks, our inevitable silences punctuated with heat and expectation. His eyes were dark and engaging. His peach Patagonia shirt was frayed at the neckline, his jeans bleached and worn, all 20-something outdoorsy boy.

He told me I was beautiful and articulate and classy.

I loved that he wasn't entirely just tight ass and sultry looks. He was substantial and educated and well-mannered.

We left the bar and drove separately to a nearby hotel. I was so reckless in those days, unafraid of strange men and seedy hotel rooms. My entire life had been turned upside down and inside out, and the threat that I would normally feel from the opposite sex was gone.

We checked into our hotel, and then Matthew took charge. He was experienced in bed, and his shyness melted away as he undressed me, piece by piece. He explored my entire body with his hands and his lips, and then he fucked me hard—multiple times—the scent of his sweat on my naked, middle-aged body, the flex of his lean, muscular body on top of and in me.

I was there, enjoying the corporeal pleasure he provided, but I was in many ways not really there at all. My body participated, but on a different plane.

I traced the outlines of his many tattoos after. *What's this one mean? And this one?* We sat together in the Jacuzzi tub and talked about the recent demise of his engagement, about how Charles and I had made the decision to open our marriage, about how my husband had already met multiple women. We talked about how difficult relationships are, how complex and challenging. How *forever* easily slips into *maybe another four years, maybe just another hour.*

"Do you want to get married and have kids one day?" I asked.

"Absolutely," he said. "I thought that's what I'd signed up for. Then she left."

I could feel the pain emanating from him. Watched his sharp jawline tighten with tension as he talked about his recently lost love.

"It's a good life," I said. "It matters. The marriage. The kids. Especially the kids. God, I can't imagine a world without them. I don't want you to think because I'm where I am in my relationship with Charles that it's not worth it. It is. Without a doubt."

He rubbed my leg in the cooling water.

I turned the hot spigot on again, felt the steam rise to my neck and into my hair, my curls responding immediately.

"I loved my husband the best I could," I said. "Our years have been really good. Mostly good. But I'm pretty sure we're not supposed to spend the rest of our lives together. I think, sometimes, the kindest and best choice is to make a different choice."

He nodded. Kissed me gently.

His facial hair felt abrasive, almost unwelcome. He made me happy for a moment, but it was all a detached physicality. Maybe that's all the happiness we can expect or hope for in this lifetime. A moment. This one. Then that one. Forever is tricky and treacherous, and there are no guarantees.

But that sweet, sad boy and his lovely mane of hair? I'll hold on to that moment for a long time. A very long time. Even though I knew when we parted that he was the last man I'd ever be physically intimate with.

CHAPTER 13

Shortly after my date with Matthew, we called a family meeting and gathered in the living room. Austin, with his bedhead; Jack, with his stoicism; Marley, with questions in her eyes. It was early afternoon on a Sunday, and we Skyped Scott in from the University of Cincinnati. He was the one I worried about the most, alone and three hours away. The other three had lived the past eighteen months with us under this volatile roof. They'd experienced the fights and the tears and the separate rooms and the storming out and the making up.

But Scott hadn't.

I looked at Scott's handsome face on the screen, his eyes still as blue as the day they pulled all ten pounds of him out of my belly. He entered this world looking more like a toddler than a newborn. He was strong and gorgeous, and he spit up more than any child I'd ever known. I used to hold him facing out so I wouldn't end up with a back full of baby vomit. We laid him out for tummy time on a giant sheet that we could change easily when it got too damp with second hand formula. I warned friends who wanted to hold him that I couldn't guarantee they'd come out of the experience dry.

"Are you hungover?" I asked, smiling at my handsome college boy on the computer screen.

"Not today," he said. "That was yesterday."

"Okay, kids," Charles began, "Mom has a letter she'd like to read you." He was composed, self-assured. We had prepared for this moment earlier, and I'd lambasted him when he'd cried again and again.

"I'm just remembering," he had explained, wiping the tears from his eyes.

When Charles and I married decades ago, we decided we'd wait five years before we started having kids. We were both establishing careers, digging ourselves out of college debt, and trying to learn to live peacefully with each other. I wasn't certain I was good mother material. We thought it best to wait until our feet were more firmly on married ground before we moved forward with a family.

Scott was born two years after we made that decision.

Then came Austin, Marley, and Jack.

Four babies in five years, our original plan thwarted.

Charles and I often said to each other in those early years, "It's all about survival." And at times, it was. Their survival. Our survival. When our babies were five, three, two, and brand new, there wasn't much time for anything else. The too-short days were made long with meal prep, nap schedules, and bath times.

"We have to let our kids have their own feelings," I'd said to Charles, twenty years later, yelling in frustration and pain and anxiousness as we prepared for this life-altering moment, for the reading of this letter that would irrevocably change all of our lives. "We can't load them down with our feelings. We have to give them room for their own experiences."

And as soon as I opened my mouth to read, I was overcome with deep, racking sobs. My voice caught, my chest cracked, the words were garbled, drowning in my mouth.

"Well, that seems an unusual way to let the kids experience their own feelings," Charles said. "Can *you* do this?"

I thought back to when Austin, our second born, came into this world and almost departed just as quickly. Those days and weeks that tested our marriage, our commitment to each other, and our gumption.

Our full-term, curly-haired, elfin newborn was in the NICU, riddled with an unknown infection, chest tubes draining his lungs, and a ventilator breathing for him. As the team of neonatologists ran tests to determine what was wrong so they could properly treat him, he got sicker and sicker. They stood by his bedside during rounds, hands on hips, shaking their heads at his mystery illness. In seventy years of combined neonatal practice, they told us, they'd never seen an illness take this particular course.

Please God, I'd prayed, *let him live. If you take someone, take me instead. He has no sins, and I have so many.*

After five weeks of agony in the NICU; after numerous late-night calls from neonatologists telling us to come say our goodbyes; after falling asleep at the electric breast pump, nipples elongated and empty; after multiple surgeries and ventilators and medications; Austin's lungs finally began working on their own.

On a weary morning after little sleep and lots of breast pumping, I took my bagged milk to the NICU freezer. My basket of milk was overflowing while others held barely any bags at all. I knew pumping was a problem for some women. It was not a problem for me. As I placed the bags beside my overfilled basket, a nurse looked at me and said, 'Oh, *you're* the one." Apparently, I had become a milking legend among the NICU nurses.

"Many marriages don't survive the NICU," we'd been told by Austin's day nurse. But we had. Our marriage had survived so much.

Until now.

I looked lovingly at each of the four humans who have taught me more about life—theirs and mine—than I could have ever imagined. I didn't know I was meant to be a mother until I became a mother.

Sometimes, when I lie in the darkness between sleep and waking, I can still smell the intoxicating scent of sweaty baby heads. The moment I open my eyes, it's gone, but the memory remains, right there beneath my chest, where the possibility of each of them first came to fruition.

I can do this, I thought to myself. *I can do anything*. These were my beloved kids, and I would always be there for them, no matter how many turns our lives might take. I nodded my answer to Charles's question, continued crying, and began reading my letter to the beautiful, smart, talented children we'd ushered into this world together.

Your dad and I have something to tell you.

But first, there is something I want to remind you.

Each of you grew under my heart—from the day you were conceived until the moment you made your way into this world. You are the best pieces of both of us, the boldest, brightest, shiniest parts. We love you unconditionally, forever. Nothing will ever change that. Nothing. You are always safe in and under both of our hearts. Forever.

Your dad and I also love each other. We have always and will always love each other. We have stood side-by-side for twenty-eight years through sunshine and storms. We have deep and abiding respect for each other, for the humans we both are individually. There is nothing either of us would change about the last twenty-eight years.

And we have many more years ahead—both of us. It's important that we live authentically, that we live fully, that we live our truest lives ... both for ourselves and as an example to you.

So what I need to tell you is this: I am attracted to women, not to men. Both your dad and I have always known this on some level; it just took me multiple decades to own and embrace it. The labels are a little tricky for me, but the reality is not. This is who I am.

When Marley was an infant, Charles took his first administrative position in Millwood, Indiana. We moved from the family farmhouse to a three-bedroom upstairs apartment. As soon as we were settled in, all of the kids got chicken pox. For two months, I was quarantined with three little ones as Charles acclimated to his new position.

A year later—at my urging—he applied for and got a position with Zanesville Community Schools. We moved again and welcomed Jack to our new Zanesville home.

It was a crazy, tumultuous time, but I did what all good wives do: I encouraged and supported my husband and his career path. And even though it was hard to give up my own career dreams, I loved the opportunity to stay home with my babies—much more than I ever imagined I would.

As our children grew and prospered and learned how to read and ride bikes, our lives fell into a predictable pattern.

We lived in a suburban neighborhood chock full of heterosexual couples like us who raised white, well-dressed kids like ours, attended youth soccer and t-ball games on Saturdays, repainted their shutters every four years, and mowed their lawns every Sunday morning after church clothes had been changed into play clothes.

It was not a bad life. It was, by many accounts, a very good one. We were overrun with Disney-themed PJs and stuffed animals and toy trains. I signed hundreds of permission slips, chaperoned field trips, and faithfully attended high school basketball games with our grade school kids properly dressed in Zanesville green and white. We took driving vacations to Florida, to Tennessee, to Kentucky. We camped and hiked and collected ticks in shady forests and seashells on faraway beaches.

But there was something about the skin of suburbia that never quite fit me.

I developed a taste for Cabernet Sauvignon and Malbec while Charles refined his bourbon palate. We drank to excess on the weekends and sometimes during the week. It was a joke among our neighbor friends that Charles only got lucky when I was the right amount of drunk.

"My window of opportunity is small," Charles would bellow, always the loudest at every party. "Katrina needs to be drunk enough to want me, but not so drunk that she wants to sleep more than she wants me."

When I would indicate my readiness to go home, he would holler, "Gotta go, friends! My window is closing quickly!"

Everyone would laugh, and we'd go home then and have drunk sex, depending on whether the window had slammed shut or not. Sometimes I'd cry during sex, sometimes I wouldn't. Charles was a generous and attentive lover.

I was a tearful one.

It was too hard for me to look at my sexuality in the sober light of day, so we just continued on, raising good kids, getting drunk, and trying to make a meaningful life.

We both knew it, though. On some cellular level, we knew.

Charles often asked the same question in different ways: "If you're going to leave me, you're going to leave for a woman, aren't you?"

The answer was one I couldn't even consider, not then. The silence in the air between us was thick with *what ifs*, but we did not address them. I did not address them. My answer to his questions was to not answer, denying nothing and allowing room for anything.

My deepest connections have always been with women, even though I loved your dad with everything I could. And your dad is the only man I've ever truly loved. But there have been women in my life since I was young. I buried those feelings and hid those experiences because I grew up in the 70s and 80s ... and I was Catholic ... and I had disapproving family members ... and I was afraid ... and confused ... and your dad held me safely from the time I was 17. He would continue to hold me safely—that's the kind of human being he is, but it's not fair to either one of us to just have pieces of the other. I want your dad to experience someone who is able to embrace him fully, unconditionally, with every ounce of being. He wants the same for me.

Your dad has met someone here in Ohio that makes him feel happiness and hope again. And I'm in contact with a woman in New York who makes me smile. She and I haven't met yet, but I hope we will soon. We are all feeling our way through this as carefully as we can.

And here's what we promise you: our love for each of you will never, ever change. No matter what other relationships we may someday have, Dad and I will always be a part of each other's lives. We have plans to dance at your weddings and hold our grandbabies and spend our holidays with all of you ... and whoever else may be a part of us then. We choose to see this equation as addition, not subtraction.

More than anything, we love you kids unconditionally. Our greatest goal is to make sure you're happy and comfortable and supported in whatever capacity you need. We are always here for questions, for concerns, for hugs, for you.

When I finished, I looked at each of them individually, gauging their responses. Scott stared into the distance in his apartment bedroom, fat tears rolling down his cheeks. His pain pierced the deepest parts of me. Austin sat stoically on the couch, looking ahead at no one, his feelings suppressed in a familiar place.

"Are you boys okay?" I asked.

Nods from the older two. "Yes, Mom, we're good."

Marley wiped a tear from her eye and said, "I love you, Mom. I'm so proud of you and so happy for you."

Jack looked at me with his half-cocked grin and said, "Damn, Mom, your memoir is going to sell a billion copies."

There they were. All four of them. The boldest, brightest, shiniest pieces of us.

* * *

Telling the kids was the most difficult thing I'd ever done. The next most difficult? Telling my mom. I didn't even know whether I should tell her or not. After all, she was 76, in a nursing home, in a wheelchair, sometimes confused from all her medication, unattached to social media. The only way she would have found out was from someone else. And that's exactly what I didn't want to happen. I had to tell her myself.

"I'm going to tell my parents in person," Charles said. And he drove to Indiana to make that happen. There in the morning, back in the evening.

"How did it go?" I asked.

"They just want us all to be okay," he said. "Dad told me he was sorry that I was hurting, and I told him it was important that he understood that you didn't hurt me. That you were just being true to you. That I was sad the life we had once planned was no longer, but that we didn't inflict that pain on each other."

"Thank you," I said, unable to think of anything else to say.

Later that week, I went to visit Mom, and it didn't go well.

She asked me in her soft, shaky voice, "Have you always been this way? Did you always know?"

And I said, "I've always been this way, but I didn't truly know or understand it until now. Looking back, I know I always felt different. In fact, I used to think about it as my 'strange feeling' when I was a kid—that feeling of being not quite like everyone else."

"Why did you get married to a man and have kids then?" she asked, and my heart split.

"Oh, Mom, that's such a hard question to answer. Maybe having my kids was the reason why I didn't understand myself until now. Maybe I was supposed to be their mother, and marrying Charles was the way to make that happen. I will never, ever regret having my kids," I said. "They were the very best things that came out of leading the life I thought I was supposed to live. I tried my best to be a good wife for Charles and for the kids. But at the core of me, I am something wholly different. Charles deserves more, and I do, too, Mom."

"Is it something I did or didn't do?" she asked.

"Of course not, Mom," I said. "You are the best, most supportive, most amazing mother I could ever ask for. I just grew up in a place where being me wasn't really an option. And that wasn't about you—that was about geography and religion and what I understood to be 'the right way' to live a life."

She shook her head slowly. "I'll always love you, Trina, but I just don't understand."

I didn't need her to understand. I just needed her to love me. I understood that what I was telling her had to be unsettling, devastating even, the rearrangement of her image of me, her idea of who I was. She must have felt on some level that she was talking to a stranger. She knew and understood me as someone for forty-six years, and now I was telling her I was someone else. I needed her to know that I wouldn't have changed a thing about the last twenty-eight years of my life, though. That Charles and I made the best of what we could under our circumstances. That our decisions had produced four amazing human beings, the crowning glory of my life. That being a mother to those four kids was a choice I would not change. Not in a million years. Not in a million lifetimes.

That's what I wanted our friends to know and understand, too—both the ones who stood beside us and the ones who chose sides, even when we never asked or wanted them to change sides.

I wanted them to know this, too: that the thought of never having to have sex with a man again—ever in my lifetime—was the most freeing and liberating experience I'd ever known. That it had nothing to do with Charles and everything to do with me. That the thought of living my life with the sweet softness of a woman and diving deeply into the feelings I'd had for so many years for those who think and look and feel like me was a revelation and a relief. That finally claiming my true identity so beautifully and so completely released me from all the expectations—real, implied, and imagined—that had plagued me for forty-six years. That I had become a winged creature, a butterfly, a bird. That I was freed from *what I thought I should be* to live *what I am*. That although it may have looked selfish from the outside, it was truly the most selfless thing I'd ever done, this release. Now we were all free to live our truths. To be fulfilled. To move with clarity into the *what next*.

CHAPTER 14

As much as I wanted to for myself, for Charles, and for the kids, I could not embrace Jess. There was something about the speed and intensity of their relationship that made me feel uneasy, replaced. Charles had promised to always love and support me—especially through this new transition—but the minute Jess made her way into his life, that changed. I wanted to be happy for him. I truly did. But I needed some time, and he did not give me that luxury. He'd been given many months to accept my sexuality, months of counseling and crying, of trying to understand and be understood. But with Jess, it all happened so suddenly. And seeing his car at her house night after night was a punch in the gut.

When we began to expand our dating lives, he told me he wouldn't date anyone with kids, that he'd raised his own and was finished with that life. But she still had three boys at home. He promised me he wouldn't date someone local. But she lived just miles away. I saw her all the time, at the grocery store, at school events. I had to figure out a way to exist in the same small town, and I wasn't sure how to traverse it. All I know is that I didn't do it well.

I was not gracious with their relationship. I was hurt that he could flip that switch so fast, that he moved on so quickly and so completely. And, of course, I could not forgive her for breaching the sanctity of our shared home.

"I told her it was okay," Charles said, always defending her. "I told her you were okay with it. If you want to be mad at someone, be mad at me."

"I *am* mad at you," I said. "But she's a grown woman who's capable of making her own decisions. And she chose to come into a married woman's home to have sex with her husband. You may talk about how wonderful she is, but I will never forget that that's how it all began."

"Our marriage was only a legal contract then," he said. "Our relationship was already over."

"But we were cohabitating for the kids," I said. "That was our shared home, our safe space. She chose to make it unsafe. What kind of woman does that?"

"She's a good woman, Katrina. The best human I've ever known."

He looked into my eyes when he said that last line, making sure I understood what it meant.

He could not, would not try to understand what that single transgression had cost us. And he could not forgive me for not readily accepting her.

She and I communicated via Facebook Messenger for a time, trying to cut through our assumptions about each other. It began with me in a fury when her aging mother "friended" me on Facebook. The notification had taken my breath away.

With shaking fingers, I typed this message to Jess: *Please tell your mother that I'm not interested in accepting a Facebook friend request from the mother of the woman who's fucking the man I'm still married to ... the same woman who willingly fucked him in the home we were sharing with our four children. Thanks.*

I was seething with anger, childish in my passive-aggressive communication. Jess responded with an apology and assured me that her mother didn't understand the nuances of social media, was probably looking at my profile, and accidentally hit the friend request.

She and I communicated a little bit more online, and she explained that she had never meant for her existence to cause me any pain.

I responded: *It's not your existence that causes me pain, it's the choices he has made with you that cause my pain. He told me he would stand with and support me through this transition, that he could not be with anyone else for a long, long time ... and when we barely had our rings off, he brought you into our shared home for sex. And then the lies began. And the anger. And the cold withdrawal. I'm sure you're a lovely person—I see warmth and kindness in your smile. But for me, you will always be wrapped up in that original betrayal, in that realization that he was not the man I thought he was. I cannot yet separate it. Hopefully, I'll be able to someday ... especially if you stay together ... especially for the sake of my beloved children. Thank you for explaining about your mom. It was another gut punch to add to the rest. It felt—once again—like an intentional, planned, manipulative way to stick a finger in a very open wound. I'm relieved to know that's not the case. I vacillate between wanting to meet you and wanting to run far, far away. I've seen you in town, and it rips me in two. It's hard to live in the same spaces. I hope that in time, I am able to separate you from the initial pain and betrayal he inflicted and be able to know you as an individual. I have to learn to trust again. He broke that in me.*

I shared that communication with Charles.

"You want my support?" he asked. "You want me to be there for you through this transition? Then you need to support me. You need to accept that Jess is a part of my life now. That's all there is to it."

"It's not so black and white," I said. "I need some time and some space. It all just happened so quickly. You told me it would be a long time before you could be with another woman, and *bam*! She's a part of your daily life within weeks. I feel blindsided."

"Things change, Katrina," he said condescendingly. "I'm finding happiness in my new life, and if you can't accept that, then we can't be friends moving forward. Friends support friends. Friends celebrate friends' happiness. That's how it works."

"I just need some time, Charles."

"It's too late for that now," he said.

As more time passed and I felt I was closer to being ready, I thought it would be in everyone's best interest if Jess and I met. If she was going to be a part of my children's lives, I wanted to know her, and on some level, I wanted her to know me. It was a first step toward eventually accepting that relationship, one of the final steps in letting Charles go.

Jess and I texted each other as we worked out plans.

She suggested drinks or coffee with or without Charles. She assured me she wasn't horrible and she wasn't perfect, either. She said she was probably navigating things ungracefully, and she didn't want to hurt me.

I responded: *I would like to meet, and I'll do my best not to chicken out and cancel. First, just you and me. I'm not ready to see the two of you together yet. Baby steps. Thanks for being so open and honest.*

We traded potential dates and times and landed on a Saturday night dinner. The Friday before, after much angst and many tears, I sent this message: *I can't meet with you tomorrow night. Here's the truth—your existence and your relationship with my husband does cause me pain. An intense, agonizing amount of it. And although he says we're husband*

and wife "legally only," he's still my husband. Couple my pain with Charles's lies and half-truths, and meeting you right now feels incredibly precarious to me. I'm not ready yet. The reaction in my gut when I see his car at your house tells me that. I can't leave this town yet because my kids are here, and yet you—and he—are around every corner ... in the town I am stuck in for the next three years. It breaks me in two. I know I'm not in an emotional place to be neutral with you. I am broken right now. He succeeded in breaking me when he promised he'd stand beside me and chose you instead. I have to heal first. Be well.

After the sex date at our house, I understood that I could no longer reside in that physical space. I could not live in a house where Charles's girlfriend visited, where they had sex when I was away. I could not read on a couch where they had cuddled and kissed. I could not wash the sheets on the bed where they'd been together. It was too soon, too much, too close. Although we had promised our kids that we wouldn't sell the house or make them share two spaces, I could not sleep in the house where he'd consummated his new relationship.

We had been planning a garage sale to downsize and split our belongings while we both looked for less expensive rentals. One for me. One for him.

The work of deciding who gets what when decades worth of shared lives are split is soul-crushing. Who keeps the stuffed Paddington Bear that Scott slept with as an infant, worn so thin you could see the stuffing? What about the blue bunny that laid across Austin's chest as the NICU ventilator kept his lungs working? And Marley's beloved Moosey Moosey Moo Moo #2? (For the record, there was never a #1.) And Jack's LEGO sets? The ones he'd spent so much of his youth building, dismantling, and building again, small hands working with great precision and intensity?

I had never been one to attach myself to things. But the things my kids were attached to was something entirely different. Beloved baby blankets, frayed at the edges and aged with use. Carefully crafted holiday gifts from their elementary school parties. Christening gowns, matching PJs. It was too much.

"I'd like to keep all the antique furniture from my family's farm," Charles said.

"I guess that's fair," I said. "Then I'd like the Pottery Barn bed and my Granny's writing desk."

We claimed the things we wanted most, negotiated what we both desired. And the rest, we moved to the garage, labeling the pieces of our lives with price tags. How much do you charge for a rocking chair that lulled your babies to sleep with its gentle movements? What's the price on a Crock Pot that fed your little ones on so many cold nights? Once you removed your wedding and family photos from the frames that held them for so many years, did you throw them away? Did you sell the frames? Was that a sacrilege of some sort?

* * *

The night I sent Jess the text telling her I could not yet meet her was the weekend of our garage sale. When Charles arrived from her house at the sale Sunday morning, there was anger emanating from every square inch of him.

He threw his Volvo into park and marched toward me with vitriol in his eyes.

"Fuck you for not letting me have anything good while you get everything you want!" he yelled at me.

"What in the hell are you yelling about?" I asked as I stopped arranging the remnants of our life on the U-shaped driveway.

"Jess broke up with me," he screamed. "She broke up with me because of *your* message!"

"Jesus Christ, Charles," I said. "That's not my fault. I didn't ask her to break up with you. I just told her I couldn't meet her yet."

"Yeah, but she's too kind to cause you the pain you *claimed* she was causing you!" he screamed.

"Oh, for fucks sake, Charles, that's on her, not on me. I didn't ask for that. And you know exactly how I feel. This shouldn't be anything new to you."

"You can't let me have anything!" he screamed, stepping closer and closer to me. "You have to suck every ounce of joy out of my life because you're a selfish bitch! You get everything you want! You got Cecilia. Now you have Lily. I have nothing!"

Charles's eyes, clouded and dark, scared me. I had never seen him so angry, with all of his energy directed at me. He'd scream at me when we were young, but he would punch walls and windshields to relieve himself of his pent-up rage. This felt like something very different.

"Fuck you for being so fucking selfish!" he yelled.

"Charles, the entire neighborhood can hear you," I said. "Stop."

"I don't give a shit who hears what," he screamed. "Everyone should know what a selfish, self-centered bitch you are! The world doesn't revolve around you, Katrina. You're not the center of the fucking universe, even though you exist like you are!"

He moved closer and closer to me, and I could feel the energy pouring off of his body like a wave of heat on asphalt.

"Leave me alone," I said, backing into the garage. He was scaring me, and I didn't know how to handle that feeling.

"Fuck you!" he screamed as he put his hands solidly on my shoulders and shoved hard.

I stumbled, but I didn't fall completely down. I ran into the house, and he followed me closely, shouting about the horrible human I was.

"I swear to God, if you touch me again, I'll call the fucking cops," I said, holding my phone up.

"Do it!" he yelled. "Go ahead! You think that scares me? Fuck you! You don't scare me, you miserable bitch!"

His breath was hot in my face, and his eyes were wild.

I ran past him, out the front door, and jumped into the Navigator. His car was blocking my exit, so I turned the wheels into the grass to get away.

"Why don't you drive that car all the way to New York and fuck your new girlfriend, you reverse Oedipal lesbian cunt!" he yelled. He'd seen the online pictures of Lily and her snow white hair, just like my mom's. As I drove out of the neighborhood, shaking and crying, I could still feel the burn of his hands, the ones that used to gently rock our babies to sleep, imprinted on my shoulders.

CHAPTER 15

To finish the transition into my new life, there was one more letter to write, one more group of friends and family to tell. To complete the circle, on a cold, rainy Parkersville day with my heart pounding wildly in my chest, I sent this message out over social media:

Dear Ones, these are probably the most important words I have ever shared with you. Some of you know, some of you are wondering, some of you are speculating. Today, I'm here to clear the air, to tell the story that's waiting to be told.

One day after our 22nd wedding anniversary, Charles and I sat down with our three high schoolers and Skyped the college boy in. I'd written a letter to them because I knew I wouldn't get through the conversation otherwise. In it, I reminded them how much I loved each of them, how nothing in the world would ever change that. I told them I loved their dad, that he loved me, and that because of that love, we both knew we deserved more than the other was able to give. I told them I wouldn't change anything about the past twenty-eight years, but that we were going to take a detour for our remaining days.

And then I told them I was gay.

There was more to the letter I read them. Of course, there is always more. Life tends to be a bit more complicated and complex than we can even imagine. The kids were amazing and supportive and strong. They hugged us and made jokes and shed a few tears. Somehow, we managed to make some pretty amazing human beings. Charles and I had big plans to cohabitate and co-parent while we lived our separate lives and supported each other on our new paths.

But plans and reality don't always align.

For the previous two years, Charles and I had grappled with how to move forward—or whether we even should. We'd been through counseling. We'd experimented with many possible solutions, including opening up our marriage to other people. But ultimately, we'd recognized this as our truth: both of us deserved more than just pieces of each other. And although we'd given each other some of our very best pieces, we both understood that "most" was not enough, was not fair or equitable, was not authentic. It was not what either of us wanted for the rest of our days.

Writing the social media version of our new reality was an exercise in finding the diamond in the sludge pit. I was amazed at how watered-down and benign I made our reality sound when our home was a ticking time bomb of uncontrolled rage and tears. Charles and I were at odds all the time, and I worried about the kids every second of every day. *Was I ruining their lives? Were they going to be okay? Could they survive the stigma of the gay mom who left their dad?* In the midst of all these changes, Marley said to me, "I never wanted to be one of *those* families." Those nine words still haunt me to this day. We were never supposed to be one of those families. We were supposed to stay intact, enviable, and happy, happy, happy.

Charles and I have made many missteps over the past few months. We have spoken harsh words. We have hurt each other. We have apologized. We have rinsed and repeated. This is not an easy journey. Twenty-eight years is a long, intersected time. There is much to unravel. But we are trying to be the best we can be so our kids have space to be the best they can be.

My sad, sweet mom—when I had the hardest conversation I've ever had with her—said to me, "But if you've always suspected you were gay, why did you get married? Why did you have kids?" And my answer remains the same ... because I grew up in the Midwest. I attended a Catholic school and was raised by a very Catholic family. I was told from my earliest days what was expected of me—not necessarily in so many words, but in everything I read, heard, ingested, viewed, and lived. And I met a boy who loved me. He told me he dreamt about me sitting in a rocking chair, holding his babies. And I loved him back ... in many good, true ways. And the thought of the silences and stares and judgment was harder to bear than the thought of white picket fences and puppies and the suburbs.

* * *

"Number nine," Sister Victoria Agnes, my elementary school religion instructor, said, "is *thou shalt not covet thy neighbor's wife*. Who can explain what that means?"

Jody's hand shot into the air, a smug grin on her face. She stood beside her desk and smoothed out her plaid jumper with her freshly manicured nails. Jody and her mom got their nails done together regularly. I didn't even know what a manicure was. I glanced at my own nails with their soft, jagged edges and red, tender cuticles. I wondered how long Revlon's Golden Ginger would hold up against my basketball, my baseball glove, and my nervous cuticle chewing habit.

"It means a man shouldn't even *think* about being with another man's wife," she said. "It's a sin to cheat in marriage, but it's also a sin to *want* to cheat."

"Thank you, Jody," Sister Victoria Agnes replied. "Yes, the ninth commandment is about covetousness and the sanctity of marriage. It is similar to the sixth commandment, but number six is about the *act*, and number nine is about the *thought*. Both are equally wrong in the eyes of God."

I furrowed my ten-year-old brow. This was a tough one for me. So, shooting someone with a gun like the one my mom kept under her pillow for protection was just as bad as *thinking* about the shooting? The former definitely seemed worse than the latter. But I wasn't God, so I didn't get to make the rules. I was just supposed to abide by them—a notion that bordered on the impossible, I thought, except for the nuns cloistered in silence in a lush, green convent setting. And even then, they were alone with their own thoughts far too frequently. Did they ever think about each other and what they were hiding under their habits? How did they keep their imaginations from running wild and their souls from blackening with sins of thought and covetousness? Was there a trick for turning your mind off? For moving from wanting my cousins' backyard pool for myself to simply admiring its aqua existence?

Catholicism is an interesting framework for a life, young or old. Immaculate conception, death on the cross, sacraments of faith, women in wimples, eternal life or fiery death.

Catholic school was both my safe haven and my place of undoing. I was hugged by the same nuns who rapped my knuckles with rulers. I was taught by female lay teachers who loved me, and whom I loved—sometimes a little too much—in return. We were all held by a God who sent His only son to save us, but still expected us to confess our sins to celibate strangers in black.

Forgive me, Father, for I have sinned.

The Confessional was both a frightening and liberating experience for me. I didn't want to tell Father Richmond all my sins. There were many—and I wasn't entirely sure where mine ended and where others' began. But it was such a reassurance to have my soul cleansed, sparkly and new. When I returned from that dark and foreboding closet with a brand new soul, I was extra careful not to fuck it up instantly with the black marks of mortal sins. I didn't talk or pass notes to my friends in the church pew. I tried to keep my thoughts from straying to cute girls, to ponder the Big Red gum I would invariably steal from Hook's Drugs later that week when I picked up Mom's cigarettes. And I squeezed my eyes shut and folded my hands tightly in front of my face to erase all thoughts of Becca from my mind. I tried to simply be grateful for her friendship. To not think about how pink and full her lips were. To not dwell on how many inches of her long, lean legs her favorite cutoffs revealed.

"If I drew a line around this classroom with a pencil and then marked one point with the sharpened edge," Sister Victoria Agnes said, "that represents the significance of your life in God's greater plan. And yet, He knows every hair on your head, every freckle on your face."

I had a lot of freckles and a great deal of unruly red hair. That seemed like too many unimportant details for God to be bothered with. Shouldn't my life itself have more significance than my follicles?

None of it made much sense to me, but Sister Victoria Agnes assured us that it was as it should be.

"Faith is believing without knowing," she said.

But I was without faith.

I wanted proof.

Just a little something, God, I prayed at night. *If You're real, let my Crissy doll come to life. Just for a minute.* But He never did. When I was angry or hurt or pissed that we had nothing while my cousins had everything, I'd expand my requests. *When I bury this quarter, let it grow into a money tree. Bring my dad back. Get my mom a new car—one that's not rusted through the bottom so she doesn't have to look at the road while she's driving over it.*

But He remained silent.

And I remained skeptical. And afraid.

* * *

I continued my social media post:

I wasn't brave enough to be me in a world that told me I should be someone else.

And the silences and stares and judgment that I feared have come to fruition, multiple decades later. What I was afraid of for all those years has become reality. I feel the empty spaces where friends used to be. I hear the silences where laughter and conversation once existed. I miss the invitations that used to come fast and furiously. I see the confusion in my mom's eyes. It's the hardest juxtaposition of all. For the first time in my life, I finally feel at peace and completely comfortable in my own skin. And yet, there is so much fallout.

There is guilt.

There is blame.

I made a beautiful family, and then I broke it.

I know those pieces will someday reassemble into something new and different and more authentic. I believe that what rises from the ashes will be even better because it will finally be the truth. My truth. But today, there is heartache and confusion tucked into the cracks between the joy and peace and contentment.

The other thing I know for sure is this: I wouldn't change one thing about my past, about the decisions I made twenty-eight years ago ... or about the decisions I've made today. Because no matter what else we might have done wrong, Charles and I did four things so very right. Their names are Scott, Austin, Marley, and Jack.

I'd written a lot about my kids when they were toddlers. I maintained an online blog where I documented their funny antics and their amusing stories. But writing about them as they grew up and older felt invasive and wrong. They were becoming independent human beings with lives of their own, and I didn't want to dictate, diminish, or assume I understood their individual experiences. Especially now. But I knew for certain that I would always consider them my life's biggest achievement.

And for those who are wondering and searching and questioning the truth of their own lives, here's the other story I want to share: Once upon a time, there was a little girl who grew up safe and loved and cocooned in the arms of her mother and big sister. She loved the girls in her life far more than the boys. She kissed her female cousins innocently in closets, giggling and discovering. And when she turned double digits, she learned from a man who should have known better that her purpose on earth was to please men, to serve them, and to stay quiet about the details. She learned from her society and her religion that loving girls was wrong, even though no other love felt quite right. She learned there was a path she was supposed to follow, and she followed it. Then multiple decades later, she learned that life is too short to live for someone else or by anyone else's rules and standards and expectations. It was the lesson she wanted to leave for her children, for the man who had held her safely for so many years, for all the little girls and boys who still wonder ... Am I doing what is expected of me? Or am I living what matters most to me? The little girl who followed the path she was supposed to—simply because she was supposed to—doesn't have regrets. Just a story to tell ... one that took a long time to learn and accept and understand. And it goes like this:

Love wins. Whatever love feels right, no matter who might say it is wrong. And the story—even though it might not have the ending she expected and envisioned—will still have a happy ending. Because the final sentences will be these: she loved. She loved well. She loved honestly. And with her whole heart. And she finally—finally—learned to love herself enough to live her truth.

The beginning.

* * *

I had high hopes when I posted my coming out message online. I thought for sure that my friends and acquaintances would understand, that they'd embrace me with open arms, that everything once muddy would clear up from the cleansing of my heartfelt words.

And many did listen and understand. But not all. There is so much fallout that exists when you end a marriage. Some of it, you expect. Some hits you with a stiff, cold wind and steals your breath away.

I found out one of my best friends, Linda, had invited Charles and Jess to a neighborhood party in Indiana, one that included all our old couples' friends. Charles and Jess had gotten back together once the fallout from the garage sale incident had settled, and Linda's invitation had come shortly thereafter. It was a gut punch to see the party play out on social media. I asked Linda why. Why had she chosen Charles and Jess and not me?

"We all love you, too," she said. "This isn't about choosing."

"But you did choose," I said. "You very clearly chose."

"Kat, this isn't easy for anyone. We all still love you."

"Then why not invite me, too? Why not let us all be adults together?"

"It's complicated," she said.

The next day, I saw that Linda had "friended" Jess on Facebook.

"Really?" I asked her. "It's not enough to have a sleepover with her at your house? Now you have to be her BFF online, too?"

"I don't understand where this is coming from, Kat," she said. "I love you. No one will ever replace you."

"But did you think about how it might make me feel, seeing you all laughing and having fun together? Do you see how that feels like an abandonment? Like a replacement?"

"No, I don't," she said. "She is not you. She will never be you. You are not replaceable."

She didn't understand. No one really did.

Going from the heterosexual status quo to the homosexual outcast in your own familiar space is challenging on numerous levels. Not only do you give up your heteronormative privilege, but you sacrifice the safety and comfort of living in the majority.

Charles never really understood, either, when I tried to explain it to him—why it was so hard on me when he jumped headfirst into a new relationship after he swore he'd stand with me through this transition. Not only did I need to grieve our marriage, but I had to figure out how to be a gay woman in a very straight world. All he had to do was find someone else. And once he did, he was gone. Physically. Emotionally. All those promises of love and support went, too. He could not hold pieces of his old life, of me, if I wasn't willing to embrace his new life, his new love. And I wasn't ready. I couldn't do it. I did not yet have the capacity.

One of my most profound losses came from one of the most unexpected places. My friend, Mia, and I were thick as thieves. She'd once bought a couch and named it "The Willis" because she finally had a piece of furniture in her cute, cozy home that fit our entire family. She transformed her guest room into a welcome oasis when I was traveling to Indiana from Mississippi. Our families vacationed together. We experienced "red wine incidents" together. We laughed until we cried.

And then she went silent.

In my overwhelming sadness, I sent her this message: *I don't know what went wrong between us, but I miss you. No matter what happens or what the future brings, I want you to know how much I love you, how much you helped shape my life during the years of our friendship. There will always be a special place in my heart reserved just for you.*

She responded: *God, don't be so dramatic. It's not like I'm dead. Friendships wax and wane. That's what's happening with us. That's all.*

It was another gaslighting; another way of telling me that I wasn't feeling what I was feeling, that my experience wasn't valid, that I was overreacting. But the silence continued, uninterrupted.

A couple years after that final text, I saw Mia while I was having dinner with my friend, Klara. We were at a restaurant that was a favorite of mine, dimly lit and intimate, and Klara and I sat at a two-top by the bar. In the back was a table full of Mia's friends and former colleagues. They could clearly see us in the elevated bar space. I recognized many of their faces as they turned their heads away from me quickly and awkwardly, like anxious middle schoolers who didn't know what to do with the strange new kid in the cafeteria.

Klara and I ordered a bottle of Cabernet to share, and as the server delivered our wine glasses, Mia entered through the front door. She walked directly past our table—head held rigid and high—and pretended she didn't see me. Eyes forward, focused on her destination, I could have reached out and grabbed her hand, she was so close. But I didn't grab her hand. I didn't reach for the arms that used to embrace me in such warm, welcoming hugs.

She had erased me with her indifference.

My face caught fire, and I couldn't stop the tears that were burning at the corners of my eyes.

She joined her table of friends, and most of them continued to pretend I wasn't there. Except one. Our sweet mutual friend, Dana, came to the table to talk to me, but Mia stayed put. She didn't look at me; didn't acknowledge me. The collective table had told Dana not to talk to me, but Dana had told them there was no way she was going to ignore me.

It felt like a seventh-grade shunning. A mean girls' table. *No, you cannot sit with us, talk to us, or look at us. No, you are not worthy. No, you are not human. No, you have no right to exist in any space other than what we deem acceptable. Yes, you are taking up too much oxygen.*

Not only was I no longer Mia's friend, I was no longer even a human worth a glance, a smile, or a hello.

Tears fell onto my cloth napkin, into my Cabernet.

"Do you want to go?" Klara, asked. "We can leave."

I shook my head. I wanted to stay; didn't want to let them win. I walked by them on my way to the bathroom, head held high. I did not allow myself to sob until I was in the stall alone.

Klara watched as their cruel indifference crushed me throughout the rest of the evening. She thanked Dana for being such a good and true friend. She held my hand across the table and said, "Fuck them. That is no longer your life. And it's their loss."

Months later, when I could finally accept the truth in Klara's statement, I began to imagine building a new community, forging a new trail. I realized I had been holding so tightly to *what was* that I wasn't allowing room for *what was yet to be*—an opportunity to create a community of those who love me as is, not as was. That was too hard for many in my past—to have had a vision of me *this way* and then to gracefully accept me *that way*.

"You have to let it go," Allison said to me as I told her the stories about Linda and Mia. "You've outgrown that life. It's time to live in the one that fits you now."

I nodded my agreement. I just had to figure out how to find my way.

CHAPTER 16

I called Charles after dropping the youngest two kids off at the high school for a musical rehearsal. The evening felt lonely and heavy, and I was hoping to build a bridge, at least a small one. Maybe one of tiny, carefully placed stones instead of concrete and steel.

"Do you think we can try to be friends?" I asked.

"Do you really mean that?" he replied.

"Yes. We used to be such good friends. It feels weird to be so at odds. We talked about moving forward together, and we've become such enemies. I miss your friendship. I'd like to work on getting that back."

"Well, you have to accept Jess," he said. "Otherwise, we can't."

We wanted to be good at our separation, at divorce. We truly thought we could be. I knew I hurt him by falling in love with Cecilia. I knew he felt abandoned, devastated. I tried to right those wrongs in therapy, in apologies, in spoken remorse, before we moved on to whatever came next. But I couldn't really let go of the fact that he'd replaced me so quickly and so completely. My jealousy and pain blurred my vision, obscured all sense of reason.

"Come on, Charles," I said. "You know I'm not ready for that. You said you wouldn't be able to be with someone else right away. And you promised it wouldn't be someone with young kids—that our kids wouldn't have to 'compete' with any others. And you told me it wouldn't be anyone local so I wouldn't have to see her all the time. And then you lied to protect her, and it made everything feel very, very unsafe. And you don't get or understand that. You just want me to accept your relationship blindly without even acknowledging how painful all those choices were. I'm not ready."

"Right," he said, his voice becoming cold and hardened. "Lots of things happen that we don't expect. I didn't plan on liking her. It happened. And I am finding happiness in our post-married life."

"You didn't plan on it?" I asked. "You very specifically chose to hook up with someone local who had young kids, and you didn't plan on it? How does that even equate? And in case you've forgotten, we're still married."

"Our marriage is a legal contract only," he said. "Nothing more."

We spiraled from there. The spiteful, bitter words came from both sides. We could not be kind to each other. We could not even be human. We used our harshest words and our meanest insults. We'd known each other for so long, we knew how and where to hit so it hurt the most.

You're nothing but a malcontent, he texted. *You will never be happy.*

I'm incredibly happy right now, I texted back. *Your anger and manipulations are the only part of my life that makes me unhappy.*

Well, I couldn't be happier, he responded. *Having your toxicity and emotional upheaval out of my life is so refreshing. Ben Folds said it best: Brick.*

That reference was about a "joke" we used to share together. When Ben Folds sang, "She's a brick and I'm drowning slowly," I would teasingly ask, "Is that how you feel about me?"

"Only once in a while," he would respond, teasing back. "No, honey, I love you. All of you. Only you." And then he would hug me. Hard.

Hug. Slap.

When I was downsized from my job less than a month after I signed a lease on a new rental home—one that would finally release me from the growing toxicity of our shared home—I texted him that I didn't know whether I would be able to contribute to our shared bills once my severance ran out. I was terrified, frantic, had no back up plan, and was stressed beyond what I'd ever faced before. I'd cried for days after I received the very unexpected call that the company I'd been with for five years was letting me go, no warning, no reason. The ground beneath me was crumbling, and I was looking for something solid and stable, something I could depend on. Charles was the one I had always depended on.

Hoping for a little understanding and compassion in a very unsettling time, I received this text from him instead: *If I have decisions to make, I'll take the Lincoln back and pay on it* (i.e., the car I was driving that was in his name), *and I'll let the VW be repossessed* (i.e., the car he was driving that was in my name). *I'll cancel your DirectTV, and I won't pay for your or Bruce's phone.*

I picked up the phone to call him. "Are you kidding me? That's your response to what I just shared with you? You're a monster!" I yelled. "This is how you're going to treat the mother of your children? You'll just let it all burn down?"

"I have no responsibility for you," he said. "That ship has sailed."

"You are so incredibly cruel," I said to him. "So selfish. And such a liar. How did I not ever see this before?"

When Charles became Zanesville High School principal years earlier, I watched as his job ate him alive. He brought fresh, new ideas to the table, and I stood by as his naysayers broke him down bit by bit. He was so smart, so dedicated, and so passionate about what he thought education should look like. I was so proud of him, and I watched as he fell into bed every night, exhausted, defeated. I watched as he tried to make positive change and was met at every turn with opposition. I remember thinking to myself, *I am going to lose him. If something doesn't give, his heart will.*

Becoming a college professor had always been Charles's retirement plan, but he moved the timeline as his career began stagnating and his spirit was squelched.

"I want to start working on my Doctorate now," he said. "The kids are young enough that they won't remember how much I'm gone."

"But *I* will," I said. "I will remember."

And I do remember, in painful twists and turns—when in his current anger and hurt he tells me how I never really supported him, how I never truly stood beside him, how I did nothing but resent and use him. I remember those long weekends when he'd leave for work on Thursday morning at 6:00 AM and not return home until Sunday night. I remember feeding our four kids on an early Saturday morning; running them to soccer, to t-ball, to basketball, to birthday parties; trying to watch a game here or there before I had to run again; arranging rides for the kids who didn't fit into my driving schedule; bathing them every night after full days, shampooing dirty hair and lotioning small bodies; throwing two or three loads of laundry into the washer every day; waking up to little voices requesting cereal, donuts, milk, or Pop-Tarts too early every morning, and doing it over again the next day. And the day after that. I remember how I'd fall into bed, utterly exhausted, praying that no one would wake up in the middle of the night with, "Mama, I think I gonna phrow up." I remember—after watching Charles get his Masters, then his Doctorate—thinking, *When is it going to be my turn? When will I get to sit in a classroom again and have drinks with my cohorts late into the evening? When will I get to talk about big, lofty ideas with my classmates? To discuss narrative arc and foreshadowing with others who cared about such things? When will I get to add additional letters behind my name? When do I get to catch up?* And when he texts me with insults now, such as *I've always been smarter than you. I will always be smarter than you* ... and *I'm not always right, just most of the time* ... I remember all over again.

But back then, when he told me that he wanted to look for a professorship as soon as he finished his thesis, I swallowed the lump in my throat and nodded. A professorship meant at least a 50% pay cut and—more likely than not—an out-of-state move. I had lived in Indiana my entire life. My family, my friends, my home: it was all right there in the Hoosier Heartland. But I loved Charles, and I was committed to him and the family we had made, and I recognized his angst, and I knew that in order to move forward together, we were going to have to embrace this adventure. And I also understood that I would have to go back to work full-time.

It wasn't my dream. But it was his. And we were partners.

When he received a job offer in Salton, Mississippi, he might have just as well told me we were moving to Mars. We visited the campus while he finished his final interviews, and I took the kids to a recommended local burger joint, The Mug and Bun Bar and Grill.

"It's a good place to raise kids, right?" I asked our poor, unsuspecting waitress through tears as ten-year-old Marley cried loudly beside me. She, of all the kids, took the news the hardest, kicking and hitting me in her blind rage in our Zanesville kitchen when I told her we were moving. "They'll be okay, right?"

"Yes, Ma'am," she said quietly. "All y'all will love it here."

Her sweet, Southern accent made me cry even harder. It was beautiful to me, and it was also a foreign language. How did I uproot everything I'd ever known and navigate it well? How did I convince these four young kids that we would be alright when I couldn't quite convince myself?

"This will be our two-year vacation," I said to Charles and the kids, but especially to myself. "We can do anything for two years, right? If we're unhappy after two years, we'll come back with great stories and a fun experience under our belts. We're the Willises. We can do anything." I was the cheerleader. The supporter. The one who smoothed all the dangerous edges.

And so we went. We relocated ourselves right in the middle of that oppressive heat, and I cried my way through the next twenty-four months.

When eight-year-old Jack came home after his first day of school, sobbing in my arms because he'd said to a teacher, "What?" instead of "Excuse me, Ma'am?" when asked a question he didn't hear and had been forced to stand humiliatingly in the corner of his brand new classroom, I knew I'd made a horrible mistake in the name of trying to preserve my family.

"Please don't make me go back there," he cried, his blonde head sweaty in my arms. "Please don't make me go back."

The challenge of Mississippi had so many sharp angles for me. I soothed my sweet Jack as he tried to navigate a school system that did not fit. Eventually, I took him out and homeschooled him to save us both from the endless evenings of tears and heartache. I counseled Marley as she struggled to find a foothold in a place that wasn't really hers, with a group of girls that never quite accepted her. Because they made friends early, the bigger boys struggled less, but there were still angst-filled moments and days for most of us.

"I can't do it anymore," I told Charles. "I know you're thriving here. I know Scott and Austin are happy. But Marley, Jack, and I aren't. We're withering and dying here."

"That's a little dramatic, isn't it? he asked.

"Not really," I said. "I can't stay here, Charles. I can't. We said two years. It will be a miracle if I make it that long."

"I'll start looking for a new position," he said. "But I can't make any promises."

"Me, neither," I said.

And that was the first time in my life it truly hit me. I could leave. I could take these four kids of mine and go home. I could take them and go anywhere. If Charles needed to stay—if this place was truly his calling—he could stay and I could go. It was a thought that had never before crossed my mind, this leaving. But once it was there, I couldn't stop thinking about what life would be like on my own, with my kids. The freedom of a new start. The opportunity to follow my own dreams, my own path, instead of someone else's. It was liberating and terrifying, this thought. It came to me in my dreams.

I worked a remote job that I simultaneously loved and loathed. I was grateful for the opportunity to contribute to our household income, but what I really wanted to do was write novels. And after penning marketing copy all day long, there were no words left in me at night.

I watched as Charles settled into his new existence as well. He grieved the demise of his former career. Some of his headiest and most progressive ideas had died a slow death, and he felt the effects of that perceived failure. But on the flip side, he immersed himself in academia with great gusto, ruminating on big ideas, eschewing a higher power as so many academics are wont to do.

Because of the shift in his working hours, we spent a lot more time together. He tried to fill the void of my family and friends, but the hole was big and deep. And our relationship was shifting as well. Charles had always loved me hard, and he had always had a propensity toward being patronizing and condescending—just enough to maintain an upper hand, to assert his authority. And as the noise and busyness of our former life fell away, the volume of those moments increased.

Insults disguised as jokes. Put-downs with a hug at the end to cool the sting. "Thanks for making dinner," he'd say. "Next time, some seasoning would be nice. Do you know what that is? Salt? Pepper?"

We ran to each other for comfort.

We retreated from each other for solitude.

And after a year and a half in Mississippi, Charles was offered a position at Bowling Green State University in Ohio, just three hours from our beloved Indiana friends and family. We found a home, packed our belongings, registered the kids for school, and moved back to the Midwest.

I thought it would save us.

It became, instead, our undoing.

I remember.

* * *

A former employee of Charles's once said this to me: "Charles and I always got along well. I was lucky. But I saw how he treated the people who didn't get along with him, and I never wanted to be on that side."

Friends who had moved from Ohio came back to visit and stay with us as our marriage was collapsing. We drank a lot of wine and bourbon, ate too much food, and laughed like old times.

When sleep beckoned, I took Tom and Jan to the guest bedroom, and I settled myself on the living room couch with my favorite pink blanket and a couple of soft pillows.

After Tom and Jan closed their door for the evening, Charles stumbled through the darkness and leaned down toward the couch, his drunken breath hot on my face.

"What do you think you're doing?" he hissed in the dark.

"What?" I asked, genuinely confused by his question.

"Why are you on this couch?" he asked. We'd been sleeping in separate rooms for over a month, but since Tom and Jan were in the guest room, I chose the couch instead. I was fine giving up the master bed for a night, but I wasn't about to sleep with Charles again. Besides, I enjoyed curling up on the couch from time to time. Its soft, ample shape felt like a warm hug.

"I'm going to sleep," I said. "You should, too. You're drunk."

"You are absolutely not going to sleep on this couch," he said menacingly. "I will not let you embarrass me in front of my friends like that."

"Oh, for fuck's sake, Charles, I'm just sleeping on a couch. Lots of people do it. Go to bed. Good night."

He grabbed my arm hard and yanked on it, pulling me toward the edge of the cushion.

"Get up," he whispered harshly. "Get the fuck up and get in our bed."

My heart started racing.

"I'm not getting in your bed," I said. "And you are not talking to me like that. Leave me alone."

"You are getting in that bed," he said.

"Leave me the fuck alone, Charles," I said, growing angrier with his drunken insistence. "I'm a grown woman. I get to decide where I sleep."

"And I'm your husband, and you're sleeping with me. You're going to regret it if you don't."

The threat in his voice made the hair stand up on the back of my neck. I grabbed my pillows and blanket.

"If you so much as lay a finger on me for any reason, I will scream," I said. "Don't test me."

I crawled into my side of the king-sized bed and jammed pillows in between us. I lay in silence with tears streaming down my face wondering how I'd been so wrong about this marriage I had committed to.

When our guests left the next day, the arguments began again.

"You're the one who knowingly lived a lie for our entire twenty-eight years together," he yelled. "But okay. You can call me the liar and the fraud if that makes you feel better. Good story. I'm sure it will make a great book someday."

"You think I'm a liar?" I asked. "You think I knowingly lied to you and raised a family in the shadow of that lie? You think it wasn't torture to try and figure out what the fuck was wrong with me?"

"I don't know how you felt, Katrina," he said coolly, slipping into the familiar ease of his condescension.

"Well, let me tell you how I feel now," I said. "I am mired in guilt for the pain I caused you and the kids. I wish I'd known who I was sooner. I wish I'd understood. But you feel nothing about the pain you've caused me in return. You're a horrible, selfish human who puts on a grand show for the rest of the world to see. Poor, victim Charles with the gay wife finally found happiness with someone else. What a happy ending. That's a great story, too."

He laughed meanly in my face. "Pain I caused you? Right! By moving forward and not carrying the burden of your emotional bullshit that you refuse to tend to yourself? You will never be happy, Katrina, because you think I—and the entire world—owe you something. You are a taker. Just like your father."

Charles was the person who knew me best. He knew the location of every wound and how to make them bleed. And he knew how much that one would hurt. The salt in my father-wound.

"Fuck you for saying that," I said, the phrase I'd never spoken to anyone before rolling easily off my tongue in the heat of our battles.

"Fuck you for living that," he spoke back.

But the battle didn't end there. For days. Weeks.

We couldn't let each other be. Couldn't stop breaking each other down.

"Go talk about it with your Fuck Buddy!" I yelled at him more than once.

"Her name is Jess," he said.

"Not to me, it's not," I yelled back.

Our rage was never-ending.

When I pointed out how cruel he was to use all my vulnerabilities against me, I texted:

> *I forgot to add the most important vulnerability to that list: my sexuality. It was fine with you when my self-discovery and eventual acceptance meant YOU got to experience threesomes and fuck women that you found online ... But as soon as I claimed that sexuality for myself, the*

narrative changed to me LYING to you, my kids, and the world. That is completely unfair ... not only to me, but to every other questioning, searching LGBTQ+ person. That's the kind of rhetoric that keeps people hiding. You want to actually be the social justice advocate you claim to be? Start there.

I was furious that his public persona was one of equality and inclusion; that his professional beliefs were founded on the benefits of public education and how every student—regardless of race, creed, sexual orientation, or socioeconomic status—deserved to be treated with equity and respect. But at home, he'd become someone entirely different—someone who couldn't support my personal transition when my sexuality didn't include him.

He replied:

Okay, sure. You see me as a user. Let me tell you how I see you as a user. You were fine using me as every form of support imaginable, but you could never really reciprocate. You would attempt to, but at the instant you were uncomfortable, that support was gone. You resented me asking you for support. You resented that we needed financial support when I made my career move. You resented that I needed emotional support. Instead of recognizing that I might need help, you told me I was crushing and suffocating you. Then you used me and my loyalty as you went on your trip of discovery. You used me as a houseboy while you ran around with Cecilia, leaving me alone. Leaving me with no answers for the questions that were swirling around. Then when you came to grips with your sexuality, you couldn't be done using me. And it was then that I truly understood who you are. The instant that I decided to take a step toward my well-being, toward my happiness, toward my life after you, you revolted. You revolted when we were supposed to be in an "open" relationship. You revolted when we decided that we would no longer be married. Anything I do that is not in service to you is met with contempt, hatred, and disgust. What you have shown me in the last two years is that you never loved me, you loved what I did for you. If you loved me, you would wish me well and let go regardless of the pain it causes. But you can't do that, either, because you have to use me one more time as the villain that hates you. Okay, Katrina. Use me as you see fit. I'm beyond feeling bad or guilty about the things you say to me. I'm numb to your barbs and jabs. You have trampled my care for you right out of me. My animosity toward you is a response to your inability to ever be happy for me. I deserve better than that and always have. I thought maybe someday you'd be able to do that but clearly not. I thought if you repaired your wounds, you'd be able to do that. I thought you leaned hard on me because you needed the support until you could have the strength to stand and then be leaned on in my times of need. But now I see it's not damage that's the issue. It's just who you are. A user. I'm done with it.

Damaged. Resentful. User. His description of our relationship, twisted to fit his own narrative, cut me to the core. I was shocked by everything he'd conveniently chosen to forget about our twenty-eight years together. I replied:

You don't even hear me anymore. But you certainly have your own narrative of how things went down ...

without any culpability on your part. I supported you through your Masters and Doctorate programs. I gave up everything I'd ever known and moved to Mississippi to support you. You forgot all the ways I tried to make it work, all the ways I supported you. Obviously, whatever I did wasn't enough, either, because I did everything wrong and you did everything right. I revolted when we opened our marriage because of your lies ... about who I was to you ... about your willingness to throw me under the bus to protect Jess ... just like I did to you with Cecilia. How can you possibly not see that? We both fucked so many things up. I admit that I fucked up more than my fair share. But all you do is blame me and own nothing. You are incapable of seeing your own contributions to the demise of our marriage. Go be happy. Apparently, that's something I was never able to give you. Thanks for pointing that out thirty years down the road. Thanks for not being able to acknowledge anything good about me or about what we had together. Thanks for recreating the story of our marriage to make yourself feel better. You've erased everything good and made me the devil. I hope that makes you feel better about your shiny, happy new life. And it's really interesting to me to hear you say NOW that I never supported you during our marriage. Why did you stay then, Charles? If your life with me was so fucking horrible, why didn't you go? And why did you get to grieve our marriage and I didn't? You were—rightfully—so angry with me about how I betrayed you with Cecilia. Why don't I get to be angry about how you betrayed me with Jess? The situations weren't the same, but you still betrayed me, my trust, what I thought you felt for me. Why do I not get to grieve that? You think I'm so fucking selfish and mean—and at times, I have been—but you don't even attempt to see how cruel and careless you've been with me.

His response?

We reap what we sow. I'm done. Business only.

There were other arguments after that, more colossal misunderstandings. We fought about him leaving the kids alone when he chose to go to Indiana with Jess instead of telling me so I could keep them with me. We fought about physical and financial care of the dogs—the ones who had been our family pets for twelve years.

But no argument really mattered anymore. When someone you spent the better part of your life with tells you that you've done nothing but disappoint him, when he admits that he thinks your character is sub-par, that you're nothing but a taker? There isn't much more to say.

There's only grief.

Hurt and fear can cause us to say and do things we wouldn't normally say or do. Charles had been my best friend. The words we so quickly and easily flung at each other during this transitional time were new and frightening.

They changed how I understood him.

I'm sure they changed how he understood me.

When I published my first book, I experienced a wave of emotions—from exhilaration to terror to imposter syndrome. As my book tour was being planned, Charles secretly compiled a video for me. In it, he'd solicited friends and family from my past and present—childhood classmates, writing friends I only knew online, neighbors, cousins, best friends—to say one word about me. Those words included: brave, fierce, love, friendship, steadfast, badass, talented, effervescent. He then set their responses to music and created one of the most beautiful, thoughtful gifts I'd ever received.

I cannot watch that video now. Some people in it are no longer in my life. Some have chosen to remain silent during our transition. Some have chosen to go. And then there's Charles at the end, calling me his soul mate, his lover. Asking me to see myself through his eyes. I have to wonder now: did he create that beautiful gift because he could feel my impending departure? Was it a final effort to convince me to stay?

We tried, one more time, to establish a friendship. I met him at The Social to catch up, to talk about the kids, to discuss the *what nexts*. We sat side by side at the bar, nursing wine and bourbon. We remained civil for about thirty minutes, and then things began to fall apart.

"What about 'til death do us part?'" he screamed angrily at me.

"You're going to throw our marriage vows at me?" I yelled back. "The ones we took in front of a God that you no longer believe in? I married a staunch Republican Christian, and now you're a left-wing atheist. Do you not think that would have ended things for many spouses? But I allowed you to grow, to change, to morph into the human being you are now—the one you most definitely weren't when we were seventeen! I supported you through that growth and self-recognition and you can't allow me to do the same?"

We threw some more barbs at each other, and he left me at the bar, crying and alone, comforted by a bartender who brought me more wine and tissues and eventually drove me safely home.

CHAPTER 17

"Allison," I said into the phone as I sat on the back patio of the home I shared with Charles, "I'm struggling." Allison had recently divorced her first husband and still juggled the two-home setup for her own kids. Charles and I had just a couple more weeks to live together as co-parents. Soon, we'd both permanently be in different homes, and our kids would spend two weeks with him, two weeks with me. The two weeks without seemed like a deep, dark cavern that I might stumble into and never emerge from. I had never been without my kids. A vacation here, a writing workshop there, but two weeks? Every two weeks? It didn't seem possible, didn't seem survivable. I craved Allison's insights, the wisdom she had gleaned from her own experience.

"I know," Allison said. "Until you're there, the unknown is excruciating. But you're gonna be okay, Kat. You will. The kids will be, too."

"I can't stop thinking about the conversations I'll miss. And the jokes. And the fights they have with each other. And their grumpiness in the morning."

"Listen, Kat," she said, "they're teenagers. It's not like they're little kids. They won't be with either of you that much. They'll be with their friends. They'll be in their rooms. They'll be making out in cars and probably smoking pot. They'll be okay."

"What if I've ruined their lives?" I asked.

"You've definitely already done that. That's our job as parents."

I gazed out at our pool and the pond beyond. So many memories had been made in that space. The kids. Their friends. Our friends. I could almost hear the laughter and the splashing and the cannonballs. I watched the oranges and pinks of the sunset sink into the water, and I poured myself a third glass of Cabernet from the bottle sitting beside me. I wrapped myself tightly in a blanket and cried silently with my best friend on the other line.

"Lily and I are starting to get deeper with each other. I've been sending her pieces of my memoir as I write them, and she's given me such sweet feedback. But we got into a huge text fight earlier today. I want to visit her, to meet her in person. She's worried about me leaving the kids, and I just want to have some agency over my own life."

"You have 100% agency over your own life," Allison said. "Look at the changes you're making so your life can be your own. You're a badass."

"I love you," I said.

"I love you," Allison said.

When we hung up, I finished my bottle of Cabernet and opened another. *Freakshow* was my current brand of choice, and the name seemed to match my internal feelings perfectly. I ran a hot bath in our oversized tub, filled it with bubbles, and took my drink and a book with me. I thought briefly about how it might feel to slip under the bubbles and not come back up. Sometimes the feelings of pain and loss were so intense, I could barely breathe. And there was guilt—so much guilt—for upending my kids' lives. All I ever wanted for them was happiness. And I was the one single handedly taking that away from them. *I never wanted to be one of those families.* Marley's sad words of defeat ran on a loop in my weary mind. I was so very tired—tired of the fights, tired of the explanations, tired of the silences from once-friends, tired of the guilt, tired of the fear. So, so tired.

I finished the second bottle of wine, climbed out of the tub, dried my pruny self, studied myself in the mirror and wondered how anyone would ever be able to love this aging body, and looked in the medicine cabinet for something to help me sleep. There, in the back corner, was a blessed bottle of Percocet with two pills remaining. I couldn't even remember what they'd originally been prescribed for—probably my back that ached constantly after I dislocated my SI joint—but there they were, my little white saviors. I popped them both in my mouth, put my pajamas on, and crawled into bed.

The second my head hit the pillow, I began crying. Hot, fat tears streamed down my face and onto my pillow. My mind was swimmy, my body exhausted. I called Allison again.

"I think I need help," I said.

"I think that's a good idea," she said. "Do you have a stress center nearby?"

"I don't know," I said.

"Kat, your speech is slurry. You don't sound right. Are you okay?"

I sobbed into the phone.

"I'm not okay, Allison. I'm not okay at all. I'm drunk, and I'm sad. I'm so sad."

The next thing I was cognizant of was Charles, shaking my shoulders roughly and yelling in my face.

"Katrina, talk to me. Are you okay?" There was no kindness in his hands or in his words. "Allison called me. She's worried about you. Did you take something?"

I nodded, but I couldn't speak through my sobs.

"Jesus fucking Christ," he said, his voice conveying more annoyance than concern. "I'm taking you to the ER."

Somehow, he dragged my limp, mostly unresponsive body to the car and drove me to the local emergency room. I don't remember much about what happened once I arrived. I just cried and cried and cried until I felt like I'd never be able to produce tears again. My eyes were so swollen, I could barely see.

"Katrina," the doctor asked, "do you want to hurt yourself or anyone else?"

I shook my head. "No, I just want to sleep. I just wanted to sleep. Please, can I go home?"

Even though I'd already expressed my wishes, the doctor looked at Charles and said, "Do you think your wife is a risk to herself or anyone else?"

He hesitated, just for a moment. He looked at me. Looked through me. Then the ultimate betrayal: he nodded his head.

"No!" I cried. "I'm not a threat! I'm just sad. I just want to sleep."

The next thing I knew, two nurses were approaching me with a set of scrubs.

"We need you to put these on," one of them said. "Can you do that, or do you need help?"

"Why do I need them?" I asked. "Please just let me go home."

"We can't let you do that," the other nurse said. "Your husband has indicated that he's worried you're a threat to yourself or others."

"I'm not!" I sobbed. "I'm not! Please, please just let me go home. I have kids and a job. I can't stay here!"

"You're not staying here," the first nurse said as she helped me undress. There was no kindness in her act, no comfort. It was all very matter-of-fact. Charles stood in the corner and watched as they changed my clothes, handed him all my belongings, handcuffed me to the bed rails like a criminal.

"Why are you doing this?" I cried.

"It's for your safety," Nurse Number Two said.

But I had never felt less safe.

"Please," I begged Charles, "please take it back! I want to go home. I want to be with my kids. I have to work tomorrow. I can't risk losing my job. Not now. Please."

He turned, instead, toward one of the nurses.

"What happens now?" he asked, his voice void of emotion.

"We're going to transfer her to a psychiatric facility that can help evaluate and take care of her. She'll be there for at least 72 hours, and the attending psychiatrist will make the final determination of what will happen after that."

"No!" I cried. "I can't be away for three days! Please ..."

But the EMTs were already there to take me away in an ambulance.

"Are you cold?" one of them asked as I shivered in my scrubs.

"Yes," I said.

They covered me with a blanket as I sobbed. I watched while Charles perfunctorily gathered my phone, my bag of clothes, my water bottle.

I began to shake, furious with him for his betrayal. He knew me. He knew I would never hurt myself. He knew I would never leave my kids. And yet he stood there, refusing to make eye contact as they wheeled me, still strapped to my bed, to a waiting ambulance that was cold and dark and terrifying. I had no idea where I was going or when I would see my kids again. I had been molested as a child and raped as a college coed, but this. This was the most violated I had ever felt.

I slept fitfully through my first night, the sheets scratchy and worn. My room was bare, empty, beige, cold. The mattress had a waterproof cover on it that made loud noises whenever I moved. I had nothing of my own with me. No book to pass the time. No journal to record my thoughts. I didn't even have a scrunchie to pull my hair back. Too dangerous, they'd said, as if I might try and hang myself with a scrunchie.

At 9:00 AM, a nurse opened my door.

"Group therapy is at 10:00," she said. "We encourage everyone to attend."

I was not attending.

Outside my door was an expansive "community room" with couches, a television, and two public phones. A woman dressed just like me walked around the perimeter of the room over and over, mumbling to herself. The other people there were mostly quiet. Some of them knew each other, some sat alone. I stayed in my room. I had no intention of getting friendly with anyone.

At 1:00 PM, the attending psychiatrist came into my room to talk.

"Tell me a little bit about why you're here," he said.

"I'm not supposed to be here," I replied.

I'm sure he heard that from most people.

"Tell me why you think that," he said.

"Because I said I wasn't planning to hurt myself or anyone else—that I was just sad and tired. Then they asked my soon-to-be ex-husband, and he told them I was a threat."

The doctor looked at me compassionately as I continued.

"We're in the middle of a divorce because I just came out of the closet after being with him for almost 30 years. He's been cruel and physically rough with me. He has a girlfriend that he brought into our home for sex. I've lost so many friends, and I'm constantly worried about my kids, and my job has been beyond stressful. I'm just trying to keep my head above water. But I don't want to kill myself. I don't want to hurt anyone. I just drank too much, and I took leftover Percocet to help me sleep. I know it was a stupid move. But it wasn't a cry for help. It was just a cry for sleep."

He smiled gently at me.

"So, you said you didn't want to be here, and it was your husband who said differently?"

I nodded.

"Can you please let me go now?"

"I'm sorry," he said softly. "By law, I have to keep you here for 72 hours. But I'll make sure to sign your release papers as soon as I possibly can. I don't think you're supposed to be here, either. If you'd like, when this is all said and done, we can talk about whether or not you want to sue the ER for coercion."

"Coercion?" I asked.

"If you said you were not a threat and you were cognizant of what you were saying, that should have been enough. They shouldn't have asked your husband as well."

"My soon-to-be ex-husband."

"Yes," he said. "That sounds like it's probably a wise move. Is there anything you need in the meantime?"

"A book? Can I have a book?"

"Of course," he said. "I'll talk to the intake nurse and ask her to contact your soon-to-be ex-husband so he can bring you some. Also, I don't expect you to join group therapy if you don't want to. I usually encourage all my patients to join, but I don't think you need it. I agree that you shouldn't be here. So, it's perfectly fine to sit here and read if that's what will get you through these 72 hours."

"Thank you, doctor," I said.

"See you tomorrow," he said. "Be strong. We'll have you out of here soon."

He closed my door as he left, granting me a bit of privacy. That evening, the intake nurse delivered me three books that Charles had brought from home.

"Did he leave a message?" I asked. "Anything from my kids?"

"No, honey, he didn't," she said, with empathy and kindness in her eyes.

I spent every minute of my time in the psychiatric ward sleeping and reading and thinking. I couldn't let myself think about my job—I had no control over what would happen there. I wondered what Charles had told the kids. I wondered if he had any regrets, or if he was enjoying the silence and ease of me being gone. Was he entertaining Jess at the house every night? I could not let myself go there.

On day two, I heard my name on the intercom.

Katrina Willis, you have a call.

I ran into the community room and grabbed the phone as quickly as I could. I cradled the receiver between my head and shoulder, trying to claim as much privacy as I could in a room full of strangers.

Lily's warm and anxious voice was on the other end.

"Are you okay?" she asked. "I've been so worried about you."

Somehow, she'd found me.

"I'm okay," I said. "Just angry and emotional and ready to be home. How did you know I was here?"

"Charles called me," she said.

"He did?" I asked incredulously.

"Yes," she said. "I picked up my phone, and he said, 'Hi, Lily, this is Charles Willis.'" She imitated him with a low, gruff voice. "I was shocked."

"Me, too," I said. "I can't believe he called you, but I'm so happy he did. It's so good to hear your voice."

"It's so good to hear yours, too," she said. "Don't worry, you'll be out of there soon. And I'm here. I'm not going anywhere."

Just knowing there was someone out there thinking about and caring for me—even if she was 500 miles away—was a warm blanket and a soft hug. I was so grateful for it, for her, for something in my life to hold onto.

PART THREE:
THE AFTERMATH

During and after a hurricane, it is natural to experience different and strong emotions. Coping with these feelings and getting help when you need it will help you, your family, and your community recover from a disaster.

(SOURCE: cdc.gov)

CHAPTER 18

The flight to LaGuardia was both familiar and unknown. I'd flown many times before, but this time, the final destination was different.

I was not going to SoHo with Cecilia, I would not be drinking Bloody Marys at Balthazar or shopping for things I couldn't afford at Bloomingdale's.

I was heading to the West Village to meet Lily in person. Nerves, anticipation, fear, possibility. All those things took residence in my heart as my Uber traversed rain-soaked New York City streets; as I adjusted my floppy, blue hat again and again.

I held her address tightly in my hand, memorizing the number: *twenty-one, twenty-one, twenty-one*. I wanted to look like I knew where I was going, even though I'd never been so unsure of my geography, of my place on this earth.

I have an air mattress, she'd texted.

I'm not sure I want an air mattress, I'd thought.

During the months we'd been texting, Lily had sent me gorgeous pictures from Provincetown, where she'd spent her summer. Candid shots of sailboats and sea and shore. I'd replied—not always in a timely manner, not yet sure of what I wanted or needed—but without fail. I couldn't shake the thought of her. Couldn't stop thinking about that lovely smile, the curl in her white hair. The nursery rhyme my mom often recited to me as a child kept running through my mind: *There was a little girl who had a little curl right in the middle of her forehead. When she was good, she was very, very good. And when she was bad, she was horrid.*

Perhaps the two of us were equally good and horrid.

Perhaps we were the perfect balance.

When I pulled up to her apartment—*twenty-one, twenty-one, twenty-one*—she met me downstairs.

That smile, in person. It lit up the whole street. She stood there in ripped jeans with a corded white belt wrapped around her little waist, and her blue eyes pierced through the rain. She smiled as I stepped out of the Uber, and she held her umbrella over both of us. The driver unloaded my overpacked suitcase, and we both laughed at the absurdity of its size.

"How long are you planning to stay?" she asked.

"You never know!" I said as we began dragging that behemoth together up to her apartment. Luckily, her neighbor came home just in time to carry my suitcase up the final two sets of stairs.

"Looks like your friend is staying a while," he laughed as he set my suitcase outside her door.

"You never know," Lily laughed in return.

"You're so tiny," I said awkwardly as we hugged inside her studio apartment, choosing all the wrong words, leaning down to minimize the six inches I had on her. *Polly Pocket*, I called her later. *Barbie shoes. Toddler clothes.* She was a little, mighty package of strength and vulnerability and a throaty laugh that was far deeper and more substantial than her physical height and her thin, muscled legs suggested.

We talked late into the night that September evening, chairs positioned across from each other in front of her unlit fireplace. I sat crisscross-applesauce, leaning forward to learn her, to memorize her gestures, the inflections in her voice, the movement of her mouth as she spoke. I had never felt more comfortable, more at ease. Two strangers, fast friends, a familiarity unlike any I'd ever known.

She was kind.

She was safe.

She was stunning.

I was smitten.

As the evening wore on, we decided to grab a bite to eat at a corner restaurant. The restaurant was packed with people at 9:00 PM, and we took the last table. We leaned into each other as we sipped our drinks and continued our conversation.

"I worry a little bit about you being on the rebound," she said. "It hasn't been very long since you were with Cecilia. I read the book, you know. I've been a rebound girl. I don't want that again. And then there's that tiny little issue of you being married—and having four kids."

I listened. Nodded. Understood. Acknowledged.

"You're probably right to be a little worried," I said. "I'm not uncomplicated. I don't just have baggage, I have a whole set of luggage—with a couple extra carry-ons thrown into the mix. But I hope you think I'm worth it, the worry, the uncertainty. I mean, nothing is guaranteed, right? You could just as easily say I'm too much and walk away. I worry, too. Maybe we can just enjoy each other here and now?"

We walked back to her apartment, and she took my hand gently in hers. It was cool and small and strong, and my stomach fluttered at her touch.

"Is this okay?" she asked.

I nodded, my heart pounding wildly.

As the night eased gently into the following day, we found ourselves yawning in between words and questions and revelations.

"So, I have an air mattress," she said as we began to talk about sleep.

I shook my head. "I don't want it. Do you?"

"No," she said. "I don't."

I felt protective of her.

I felt drawn to her.

A magnet. A flame. A luminescence.

I felt both the comfort of worn cotton and the electricity of attraction.

I was simultaneously full of nervousness and excitement—"nervcited" we'd later call that feeling—as I brushed my teeth and removed my mascara, as I looked at my reflection in the mirror, as I recognized who I was, who I'd always been. I nodded at that forty-six-year-old woman, blew her a kiss, assured her that all was well and right and good.

And as I curled into Lily in the darkness of her apartment and the white of her freshly washed sheets, as I rested my hand on her forearm, then ran my fingernails along the back of her hand, as her muscled legs intertwined with mine, as the soft of her lips and the warmth of our tongues met, all I could think, with undeniable clarity—mind contemplating, heart racing, body shuddering—was, *I'm home.*

Five hundred and fifty miles from the house in which I reside, I'm home.

* * *

A month after that first visit, we spent our second weekend together, Lily and I. It was only a handful of weeks, but the in-between felt like an eternity. When I went to bed in Ohio at night, it was her face I saw. When I woke up in the morning, it was her skin I craved. I spent the long hours of every night longing to mold my body into hers, to feel the warmth of her intermixed with me.

I could not escape the thought of her.

I could not return to her quickly enough.

What she was teaching me was this: sometimes the *real* resides in the *in-between*, in the unexpected—like *reading between the lines*. What truly matters is often not what's said, but what's implied: not the raging fire, but the spark that began the flames; not the deep intake of breath, but the steady one, the one you cannot live without. The slow, sustained burn, not void of passion or explosion or searing heat, but the entity that peels the skin from its home, that establishes the scar that remains when all the ashes have long ago blown into distant skies. The sacred, raised, calloused skin that your fingers return to time after time, to trace the outline, the path, the moment when everything was altered. Irrevocably.

It seemed an eternity passed between our first visit and our next, like a raging river that was not traversable until three miles down the path when the rocks creating the rapids sunk low and deep into their cold, wet homes. Those three miles were excruciating, but necessary for survival. The path was slick and cold, but on the other side, the glass-surfaced lake emerged.

Sanctuary.

When I returned to her NYC home, we did everything and nothing. She bought tickets for us to see The Color Purple on Broadway; the only Broadway show I'd been to since *Phantom of the Opera* in 1988. We were close to the stage, and I was mesmerized. Cynthia Erivo was pure magic. I could feel Lily looking at me to gauge my reaction throughout the show, but I couldn't look away from what was happening onstage. At one point, Lily held my hand, and I was both scared and exhilarated. But then I realized we were in NYC, where same-sex couples held hands in public all the time, and I relaxed into the warmth of her affection.

Shug and Celie sang *What About Love*, and my heart beat wildly in my chest, so loudly, I was sure everyone around me could hear it. That forbidden, unexpected desire settled in my throat and made its way out through my tears. I held Lily's hand tighter and tighter.

The next day, we walked along the Hudson River, and I saw the Statue of Liberty for the first time, the cold wind blowing through my curls. It brought me to unexpected tears, this moment. Lily's arm around me, with that iconic statue in the distance. Her cute black beanie perched on top of her tiny head, that swirl of white hair curling around the front. It was a homecoming in a million different ways. This place. The cold blue of the water. The warm blue of her eyes.

We tried on shoes (hers, so tiny next to my giant ones) and shopped for masonry nails and window blinds. We watched Chris Hayes and ate Eva's carryout and held hands and talked about everything under the sun.

I met her cousin, Harriet, this extension of her, the same blood coursing through both sets of veins. It was a sacred introduction to meet someone who shared her history, her childhood, her family, her story. When Harriet hugged me, it felt like we had already hugged a million times before. Perhaps it was a result of the shared DNA that had already crept under my skin, the heart that beat under my hand as we fell asleep in a shared bed made up carefully with crisp, white sheets.

We got caught in a hailstorm on our way home from shopping one evening, so we bought a cheap umbrella from a street vendor. We splashed through deep puddles that appeared out of nowhere. She nudged me gently in the direction she wanted me to go, guiding me through unknown city streets with precision and protection. We huddled together, arms around each other, scaffolding protecting us from the fiercest parts of the storm.

But the hail could have beaten down on my uncovered head, and I would not have felt it. All I could feel was her. The lightning. That moment. The cold. The warmth. Her hand in mine. Her breath, hot on my face. Her eyes shining in the dark. My heart in sync with the rhythm of the rain. The unspoken promise of what was yet to come. The discoveries that still remained. The life that awaited me.

CHAPTER 19

After all was said and done, after I had finally reconciled my heart, my mind, my body, my existence; after I knew what my future held, what had been missing from my past, and where my path would lead; I returned to my childhood home.

I went back to my mom in the small town where my story began. The place where, 46 years ago, my father left long before I'd made my way through the ragged emergency hole in my mother's stomach, red curls glistening, all the indignities of the world bursting from my new lungs. Aunt Maren had been there to witness my arrival and had always described it as a cut scene from *The Exorcist*, gleefully recounting how my head had twisted from side to side while I screamed all my newborn complaints to everyone in the delivery room.

"You were not about to enter this world unnoticed," my mom would say in response to Maren's story, a Merit Ultra Light elegantly balanced between middle and pointer, burgundy lipstick marks on the edge. She'd stopped dying her hair black and had let it grow into its natural snowstorm white. My mother was gorgeous with her chiseled cheeks and eyes so dark and deep a person could get lost in them and never find their way out. "No one was going to miss your arrival. Your sister, on the other hand, came sweetly and quietly. She smiled from day one, and she never stopped. You two have always been my little polar opposites."

My sister looked like my mom with her dark eyes and dark hair. She looked like my wealthy cousins, like my beloved maternal aunts and uncles. I looked like my dad, like the family I didn't really know. Red curls, blue eyes, freckles too numerous to count. I looked different. Felt different. Wished I was thin and willowy like the Applegates, not sturdy and athletic like the Harts. The Applegates, I knew; the Harts, I did not. With no one to emulate, I wasn't sure who to be.

My dad came back into our lives periodically when I was young, but he never stayed. He was a wanderer, a dreamer, a drinker, a gambler. When he was around, he was loud, fun, the life of the party. A former football player in the Marines, he was a muscular hulk with an abundance of chest hair and too many gold chains spilling out of his unbuttoned shirt. Excessive. That was my dad. A lot. The blue of his April morning eyes and the alluring space between his teeth caused many female heads to turn. Dad drank Scotch on the rocks, called me "his little shit," and breezed in on random birthdays and the occasional Christmas Eve with marketing swag he'd been given by his favorite bartenders: a neon Heineken sign, a Jameson mirror.

"I bet none of your friends have these," he'd say, his silver mustache bouncing with each word. And he was right. My Catholic school friends got tiny crosses on gold chains from their fathers. Santa Claus left them frilly dresses, golden-haired baby dolls, and tea sets under the tree. No one else had an XL men's t-shirt with Jose Cuervo emblazoned across the front. I slept in mine, the hem hanging just above my skinned and scabby knees.

One Christmas morning, when I was seven and still waiting to hear Santa's sleigh on our apartment roof, Dad arrived with rainbow striped bags stuffed full of Life Savers and Bubble Yum. I was careful around him, and a bit shy. I didn't want to scare him away with my loud voice and my aggressive freckles and my barrage of questions. *Where have you been? What did you do there without us? How long are you staying? Why did you go? What can I do to make you stay?*

I vividly recall how he wrapped me up in his arms on our worn couch while we watched TV that night. I breathed in the scent of his Old Spice and his Scotch so it would stay with me, deep in my lungs, because I knew he wouldn't. I wanted to tell him about my playground basketball team, about riding my bike to play baseball at the Boys Club. I wanted to tell him how I was the only girl on the boys' team. Wanted him to know how good I was. But what he really wanted to do was talk about himself, his dreams, his grand plans. So I listened. And I breathed him in some more. He talked about a faraway land called California and pairs of aces and balmy, palm tree sunsets. As I was nodding off to sleep, Mom took me from his arms to tuck me into bed. And I held on a little longer, not wanting to let go. I said, *Please stay.* But I only said it in my head, not with my voice.

Because I knew he wouldn't.

It became the mantra of my life.

Please stay. Please stay. Please stay.

Decades later, when one-by-one my own children were pulled from my belly, wet and wide-eyed and slippery, this was a reality I could not reconcile: the choosing not to stay. The leaving. The decision to bring a child into the world and then to walk away. It was a life I could not slip into; it was a hand-me-down dress that did not fit.

That long-ago Christmas night when my wild red curls were still unkempt and my freckles had not yet faded, I woke in the wee hours, reached under my bed, and pulled out the colorful bag Dad had bought me. I sat up against my pillows, careful not to wake Candace sleeping a few feet away, and I unwrapped piece after piece of grape Bubble Yum. I shoved it all into my mouth, chewing and salivating until I could hardly move my jaws. I let the purple spit run down my throat and down my chin as I savored the sugary, artificial grape flavor. Anything grape still reminds me of my dad and what I then understood to be a father's love—unexpected gifts of gum and candy and a few hours together in front of the TV.

Every time Dad left, he took all my oxygen with him. It was these little abandonments, these pockets of disappointment that pierced my heart again and again until it was left holey and damaged and incomplete. As I grew, my need for him was as big as my mother's stomach wound, as pink and raw as her early scar.

She wanted nothing more than to be a wife and mother.

I wanted nothing more than to be a wanted daughter.

* * *

My visit with Mom in the nursing home was filled with long silences at first. We both knew there were truths to be spoken, voids to be filled with words and explanations. But we were, mother and daughter, too timid to make the first move in our new and unexplored reality. We ate lunch in the nursing home dining room, made small talk about my kids, discussed work, the dogs, and her latest hospital reports.

When our bellies were full and her eyelids droopy, we went back to her room. She needed to rest a bit, and Bruce helped her into bed. I sat beside her, holding her translucent, paper-skinned hand, and Bruce walked to the TV room to give us a bit of privacy.

"How are you, Trinks?" she asked. "How are you *really*?"

She looked at me with her dark, knowing eyes, and I understood what she wanted to know. Of course I understood. She was my beloved mom. My rock. My heart.

"I'm good, Mom. I'm really happy. I am."

I paused.

"The day-to-day isn't always easy, and I worry about the kids all the time. I don't want this to send them into therapy for the rest of their lives. I want them to be happy and well-adjusted, and I don't want to be the cause of any pain for them. But I know in my gut that what I'm doing is right and necessary. And I hope that the kids will see that someday, too—that I was brave enough to leave a situation that was no longer healthy or right for me. When I don't get caught up in the nostalgia and the baby books and the memories, it's a big exhale for me. A huge one. It really is."

She nodded, knowingly.

"I'm looking for a little rental home in Parkersville. I'll stay there until Jack graduates from high school. It feels scary and right. It feels like my future. You know I've never lived on my own. I've never been without someone to take care of me. I want to take care of me now. It's time."

"And Charles?" she asked.

"He's looking for a place, too," I said. "He has a girlfriend. He says she makes him happy. He says she's the best human he's ever known."

Mom rolled her eyes.

"Is she the one with the gray hair?" Mom asked. "I've seen her picture. Candace showed me."

"Yes," I said. "That's her."

"She's nowhere close to being as gorgeous as you are," Mom said.

"You have to say that," I laughed. "You're my mom. But I'm still glad you said it."

"That part has been hard. Really hard," I said. "He lied to me about her in the beginning. Now everything feels like a lie. Our whole marriage. I'm sure it probably feels the same for him. I mean, his wife is gay, right? That's a pretty big adjustment. But I've seen pieces of him that I don't like, parts of him that scare me. Even if I wasn't gay, I wouldn't stay. He's revealed too much to me in the past few months."

Mom paused. Took a breath. Measured her words.

"There were many, many times I bit my tongue during your marriage," she said. "I didn't like the way he treated the kids. He was always so rough with them, dragging them out of restaurants by their little arms to discipline them for some minor infraction. It used to make me cry to watch their little legs working so hard to keep up with him. I didn't like the way he spoke to you. He could be so cruel, and he tried to disguise it as being funny. I know there was a lot of good about him, but he was also patronizing and condescending. And mean. You always defended him, and I thought that was an admirable thing for you to do as his wife. But it always made me crazy. I wanted you to speak up for yourself. I wanted to see the spunky, butt-kicking, redheaded grade schooler who defended her big sister and beat all the boys on the basketball field."

"Court, Mom. Basketball court." I laughed. As much as my mom had supported all my athletic endeavors, she never quite understood them. But she never missed a game. She and Bruce were my biggest cheerleaders.

"Whatever. You know what I mean. I missed her. I thought she was gone forever."

"She's not gone," I promised, as I rubbed her hand with my thumb. "She's right here. She's just been sleeping for a while.

She's been coasting. Acquiescing. Keeping the peace. Doing what she thought she was supposed to do."

"Tell me about your Lily," she said.

I smiled then. Caught my breath. Felt a warmth spread through my chest. Mom had called her "my Lily."

"I love her, Mom. I do. You will, too. She's kind and fun and active and exasperating and hard-working and thoughtful and beloved by her family and friends. She makes me feel comfortable in my own skin. She makes me feel equal and honored and at home. She's funny and quirky and tiny and adorable. She conducts her own private dance parties and sings off key. And she had the most beautiful blue eyes you can imagine. Like oceans upon oceans. I can't wait for you to meet her."

Mom squeezed my hand.

"I can't wait, either. Because if she makes you happy, that's all that matters. I just want you to be happy, Trinks. That's all I've ever wanted."

"I'm so happy, Mom. I'm so very happy. Like I've never been happy before."

And we hugged then. I leaned down to awkwardly embrace her in her hospital bed. I wanted to crawl up beside her, to inhale her like I did when I was little. To lay my head in her lap while she ran her fingers through my hair. But I was no longer little. I was a grown woman, a mother of four myself, a soon-to-be-ex-wife, a friend who had been both abandoned and held by others, a 46-year-old who had no contact with her biological father, a woman madly in love with another woman, a human with a future full of hope and possibility, a conundrum, a paradox, a promise.

So I just held her and breathed a little deeper and exhaled a little longer and understood that I was safe. I was loved. I was accepted.

CHAPTER 20

"I have never seen such gorgeous hydrangeas," I said as Lily pulled a suitcase (a smaller one this time) from the back of my Lincoln. I'd driven that giant gas-guzzler fourteen hours to Provincetown, Massachusetts to spend a week with her by the bay. She stuck her little head through a ring of cornflower blue blooms, and I laughed while I snapped a picture. The air was clean and smelled of salt and warmth. The sky was the color of the hydrangeas that framed Lily's head. I was so happy to be with her. I would have driven one hundred times as many miles to spend this week in her company.

We walked through her cousin's backyard, past the pool and the adjoining houses, to a little studio called the El. It was quintessential Massachusetts, and the bay was just across the street and down a flight of weathered stairs. The El itself was tiny and quaint, with a bathroom that was only big enough for one and a kitchen that was even smaller.

It was perfect.

The first evening I was there, she walked me down Commercial Street to get burgers at the Local 186. I was charmed by the rows of beautiful homes, awestruck by the beauty of the bay.

But there was something so much more.

To be in this place was like nothing I'd ever experienced before. There were gay couples and families everywhere. Men dressed in skimpy shorts and sequins, holding hands. Drag queens passing out show fliers. Women walking hand-in-hand accompanied by kids wearing rainbow shirts. It was flamboyant and fun and alive with joy. There were no sideways glances. There was no judgment, no side-eye. There was raucous laughter and loud music and acceptance. It was a life I could not have summoned in my wildest imaginings.

The following night, we had plans to eat at the Red Inn, one of the most iconic Provincetown restaurants that sat right on the water's edge. Lily was an open water swimmer, and she wanted to get her daily swim in before dinner. The timing of her swims depended on the tide, and this night, the perfect tide was right before our reservation.

"Why don't you go early to the Red Inn and have a glass or two of wine. When I'm finished, I'll take a quick shower and meet you. And if you want to see me, sit outside on the deck. I'll swim right by you."

It sounded like an ideal plan. Wine, water, a book, and my girl, swimming in the bay. I enjoyed the warmth of the sun on my shoulders as I sat in an Adirondack chair and sipped my wine, twirling the stem between my fingers. It was hard to concentrate on my book because there was so much to see and experience. The bay, the beach, the people, the vibe. There was a bustle beside me, and I heard someone say, "Look! Someone is swimming by the jetty!"

And there she was, my tiny mermaid, all alone in the water. She looked fierce and swam quickly, gliding with ease and grace, and my chest swelled with pride.

"That's my partner," I said, excitedly, feeling comfortable saying "partner" in such a warm and welcoming place. "She swims it every day!"

"She's so brave," the other woman said. "Isn't she afraid of sharks?"

"A little. Only if they mistake her for a seal. She's mostly afraid of seals, though," I said. "I guess they can be pretty aggressive."

An hour later, Lily joined me on the patio, her cheeks flushed with activity, her hair glistening in the setting sun.

"Is this the swimmer?" that same woman asked.

"It is!" I said proudly. "Isn't she amazing?" I kissed her cheek, tan and freckled from all the time she spent outside, swimming and walking and riding her bike. She was fourteen years older than me, but she was so active and fit—the most vibrant sixty-year-old I'd ever known. I couldn't even begin to keep up with her. She was always moving, always ready for the next adventure.

"And this one is a famous writer," Lily said as I laughed and rolled my eyes.

We were so happy, so proud of each other, so very smitten.

Later in the week, Lily and I planned to join a couple of her friends for a tea dance at the Boatslip.

"What's a tea dance?" I asked.

"Just a dance," she said.

"But why tea?" I asked. "Do they serve it?"

She laughed. "It's just what it's called."

I had so many questions.

Loud music, sweaty bodies, cold drinks. We smashed ourselves onto the dance floor with what seemed like a million other gays and lesbians. There were wigs and fabulous costumes and tattoos and flags. There were bodies that were cut with muscle, and there were bodies that kept dancing after the music ended. Lily introduced me to everyone she knew, and we all danced together. We laughed together. We sweated together. It was a special kind of togetherness I had never known.

Growing up Catholic in a small, Midwestern town doesn't lend itself to understanding or knowing what a gay-friendly space feels like, how acceptance can seep into your blood and make you feel human and at home in skin that has always felt like a betrayal. In Grayfield, Indiana, I knew two homosexuals. One was my mom's beloved hairdresser, Daniel. Handsome and flamboyant and outspoken, he died by suicide when I was still young. His clients adored him, but I imagine being himself in a larger community that wouldn't embrace him wasn't the easiest life to lead. The other was my volleyball coach who lived with her partner on the outskirts of town. When attending volleyball games, her partner stayed in the shadows, quiet and unassuming. They never held hands or kissed or exhibited any physical affection in public. They both knew the potential cost of those actions. Their relationship was not welcomed with open arms or embraced by our community.

In fact, the people I knew as a child never really spoke words like gay, homosexual, or lesbian. They were as taboo as some of the words we'd use to slander those of different races. Those words were so foreign on my tongue that it took me a long time to actually be able to say, "I am gay." And even now, I don't proclaim it openly. Internalized homophobia is real. There is a discomfort inside of me that settles around the edges of who I am. I never had any reservations about introducing Charles as my husband. But the first time someone introduced me as Lily's "partner," I felt my face flush a thousand shades of red. It was exciting and unknown and terrifying all at once.

There is power in naming things, though. I know farmers who do not name the animals intended for slaughter. Naming makes everything too real, too intimate. But in Provincetown, all the words were used, all the labels were proudly displayed, all identities were celebrated.

The people were gay. The shops were gay. The decor was gay. The clothes were gay. The music was gay. The shows were gay. The parades were the gayest gay I could possibly imagine. This town was a safe, gay oasis in a world full of fear and judgment and prejudice.

I never wanted to leave.

CHAPTER 21

"I'll take it!" I told my new landlord excitedly after returning to Parkersville from Provincetown. "When can I move in?"

"It's ready when you are," he said, and he handed me the keys.

I had been ready for months to move into a new place, my own place, a clean slate. I had pared down my belongings, gotten rid of everything that didn't bring me happiness, and waited patiently until the day the keys were in my hand.

This cute, quirky bungalow that stood on the corner of a wooded street was the first home I would live in without a parent, a roommate, or a partner. The main level had a kitchen, two bedrooms (one for Marley and one for Jack), and the only bathroom in the house. The basement had a finished area for Austin, and an unfinished room that housed a washer and dryer. At the top of the creaky, wooden stairs was my bedroom. It was big and bright and light with three windows, and the wooden floor was aged but beautiful. The ceiling peaked into a V shape, and there was a tiny corner nook for my writing desk. But the selling points for me were the screened three-season patio and the firepit in the fully fenced backyard. I smelled freedom in the scent of the aging trees. I saw cool fall nights with a fire, my kids, and a glass of Cabernet. Maybe Lily would visit someday, too. I would take our aging dogs, Maggie and Lucy, to live with me. They would be safe and at home with the kids and me, free to lie in the cool grass as they lived out their golden years.

"Your closet has horror movie lights in it," Austin remarked when he first took a tour. "This place is probably haunted."

"Stop talking," I said, holding my hand up to his mouth. "I won't let you ruin this for me."

"It's already ruined," Jack said, out of breath as he ran up the basement stairs. "I just saw two centipedes in the basement, and there's a crawl space that has creepy old kids' toys in it.

"Centipedes?!" Marley cried. "I can't live here with centipedes!"

But we did eventually live there with centipedes. And there were lots of them. They were the bane of my existence, but when I was upstairs, I tried to pretend they weren't lurking in the basement. Every once in a while, one would be relaxing in the bathtub in the morning in all its hairy, leggy glory, and I would lose years off my life. But this place was mine. All mine. The kids and the dogs and I had our own space.

My bed upstairs had crystal knobs on the headboard that reflected rainbows on my walls at certain hours of the day. It seemed like a sign that this was the right move.

Charles and I agreed that we would share the kids in two-week intervals. It would be less disruptive for them to have to move less often. He'd recently found a place to rent a couple of blocks from me, so they could walk back and forth whenever they wanted.

Jack and I spent many hours at Pier One, choosing a small, gray sofa and colorful throw pillows. I fell in love with a rug online, and as Maggie's age caught up with her, she ruined it in a few short weeks. I didn't care. She was our precious family pet, and rugs were replaceable.

When the kids were with Charles, I flew to New York to be with Lily. I wanted to stay the full two weeks with her, but she was reluctant.

"I'm worried that your kids will resent you for being gone so much," she said.

"But they're not with me anyway. They're with their dad. When they're with me, I'm 100% there. I'd like to be 100% with you when they're not."

It was an argument we had many times. She was anxious, and her anxiety made me feel unwanted and unwelcome. The days when I stayed in my new house with only the dogs and centipedes, I felt lonely. I cried myself to sleep more often than not. I loved the new place, loved the freedom and independence it granted me, and I learned how to mow the lawn and grill burgers. I was also plagued with guilt for making my kids share two homes when we'd promised them they wouldn't have to. But I could no longer live in a house where Jess was now a common fixture in my absence.

When I agreed to take Maggie and Lucy, I asked Charles to agree to feed and care for them when I was traveling. For a while, it worked. Then after a trip to New York, I came home to a couch that had been chewed, a rug that had been ruined, and an abscess on Lucy's foot that hadn't been treated. It was clear that they were suffering from anxiety and distress, and I was furious with Charles for his inattentiveness.

"Listen, Katrina," he said. "You can be as angry as you want to. Your anger is so common now, it doesn't even bother me. But the condition of your house is not my responsibility. I check on the dogs two times a day, and I think that's more than enough."

"But they destroyed my house!" I said. "Did you not even notice?"

"I don't even like coming into your house," he said. "I spend as little time as possible there when I come over."

"So you don't play with them or give them any company?" I asked.

"I made sure they're fed and have water," he said. "That's what I agreed to."

"But Charles," I said, "They're our family pets. Don't you care about their well-being at all?"

"They're like silverware to me," he said. "You took them, and I don't want them back. And if they're such beloved family pets, then maybe you should have the kids take care of them while you're gone instead of me. I'm enjoying my dog-free life."

They say the character of a human can be measured by how they treat animals. In that moment, I fully understood who my husband was; who he had allowed himself to become in his pain. He willingly watched Jess's dogs when she was gone, but purely out of spite and anger, he was willing to let our dogs—the ones who'd lived in our home and slept at our feet for twelve years—suffer.

After he spoke those words, I hired a dogsitter to care for sweet Maggie and Lucy when I traveled. He was unwilling to help pay for their care, but they were happy and content whenever I came home. That was worth every penny spent.

I loved cooking dinner in my tiny kitchen overlooking the backyard. My two youngest kids were vegetarians, so I experimented with meat-free meals, much to Austin's dismay. But there was something soothing and wholesome about chopping fresh vegetables that I'd bought at the Farmers Market in anticipation of feeding my growing children.

One evening, Marley was preparing to leave for her job as a busser at a local restaurant while I chopped onions and green peppers by the window.

"See you later, Mom!" she called as she breezed out the door. I watched her walk to her car that was parked in the alley behind the house. It was surreal to me that my kids were driving, working, tiptoeing into their adult lives.

I turned my head to reach for another pepper when I heard a scream that froze the blood in my veins. Dropping everything on the counter, I ran outside to find Marley holding the side of her face in her hands, blood running freely through her fingers, onto her work shirt and onto the ground.

"Oh, my God!" I cried, trying to assess what was happening. "Get in the car, baby! Use your shirt and keep pressure on the bleeding."

We climbed into her car as I yelled at Jack to call his dad and have him meet us at the hospital emergency room.

"What happened, baby?" I cried frantically as I threw the car into drive.

"It was the neighbor's dog," she cried. "The Siberian Husky. He was out of his fence, and I tried to help his owner get him back in. When I leaned down and held my hand out to him, he attacked."

Our neighbor ran toward the car, asking if Marley was okay.

"We're going to the ER now," I said as I drove off.

"Please don't let them put the dog down," she cried. "I know he didn't mean it. Please, Mom. Don't let them."

My sweet, animal-loving girl begged for mercy for the dog as she bled all over her car. I was terrified to see the real damage to her face.

"Did he get your eye?" I asked, afraid to hear the answer.

"No," she said. "Just my cheek and ear, I think." She was remarkably calm.

I ran red lights, rushing to get her help. As they whisked her away into the ER, Charles arrived.

"What happened? Is she okay?"

"It was a dog," I said. "I haven't seen the damage yet. I got her in the car and drove straight here."

"Fuck," he said as we ran into the ER together.

There was our beautiful girl, lying on a blood-stained gurney, her cheek an open wound, her ear dangling from the spot where it once held.

"Mom and Dad?" the doctor asked kindly.

We nodded together.

"We're going to need some stitches. I'm going to go ahead and try to numb this ear, although it's a tough spot for anesthesia."

I grabbed Marley's hand as Charles settled in by her head.

She cried out as the first needle pierced the tender skin of her face.

"Ouch! Ouch! Ouch!" she sobbed as my heart crumpled into itself.

"I know, Sweetie," the doctor said. "I'm sorry. I know this hurts."

He gave her a second shot, then a third, as Marley wailed in pain.

"Okay," he said as the nurse handed him a needle, "I'm going to stitch this now, and I promise I'll be quick."

"But I can still feel it," Marley sobbed.

"I know," he said. "I promise it will be fast."

As he sewed her beautiful face back together, Marley's cries of pain echoed throughout the building. The walls shook with her fear and suffering, and there was nothing I could do to make it better. It was such a helpless moment, like standing at Austin's infant bedside, willing the air in my lungs to save his weak and battered ones. But as much as we want to shelter our children from pain and fear, life inevitably has different plans. Not one of us, after all, is free from the brutality of this world. The most we can do is hold each other and love as best we can and move forward with dignity and truth and as much grace as we can possibly muster. Marley's beautiful scars are a reminder that I cannot protect her from everything else this world will throw her way, but I can choose to be there beside her, easing whatever pain I can.

CHAPTER 22

"Look at this face," I said to Jack as I turned my laptop so he could see. The Toledo Humane Society had just received seven border collie puppies from an abuse and neglect situation, and I was obsessed with their online pictures. Jack huddled beside me on the sofa as we scrolled through photos on my laptop.

"That's Prince Phillip. He's the only boy. The other six are girls. Can you even get over them?"

They were beautiful puppies, wide-eyed and silky, anxiety and fear prominent in their innocent baby faces.

"Are we getting one?" Jack asked. Sweet Maggie sat at his feet, her age evident in her white whiskers and her slow, careful steps. I had recently lined all the wooden floors with stair treads so she could safely walk from rug to rug without fear of slipping.

"Should we?" I smiled.

"Well, I think we should at least go meet them," he said.

I knew I could count on my animal-loving boy to support me in this venture.

"They're available for adoption on Saturday morning. We should be first in line," I said.

We arrived 30 minutes before the Humane Society opened, and there were already two groups of people waiting at the doors ahead of us.

"Are you here for the border collies?" I asked.

"Sure am. I want the boy," a dungareed farmer said.

As we waited for the doors to open, a huge line formed behind us.

"I guess border collies are pretty popular," I whispered to Jack.

"Which one are you going to try and get?" he asked.

"Whichever one I can," I answered.

When it was my turn to pick the puppy I wanted to visit, I remembered Cinderella's name first. The volunteer led Jack and me back to a small, quiet room where we saw a shivering black ball in the corner. Jack and I both got on the ground and inched our way slowly to the frightened puppy. She didn't look at us, didn't acknowledge us, she just kept her face in the corner and shook uncontrollably.

"Oh, sweet girl," I said, touching her gently. "It's okay. We won't hurt you. We're here to love you if you'll let us."

Her fur was long and soft. I stroked her back gently, and Jack whispered all kinds of secrets in her ears.

"Do you know what happened to them?" I asked the volunteer.

"They're an abuse and neglect case out of Mississippi," she said. "We don't know much more than that. We're pretty sure they've spent their entire lives in cages."

The puppies were approximately six months old. Six months is a long time to go without human contact, without love, without sunshine, without companionship.

"Your application has been approved," the volunteer said. "She's yours if you want her. Or you can visit with another one of the puppies if you'd like. I think she's the most timid of them all." My heart leapt at the words "she's yours." I could not imagine leaving this sweet baby balled up in the corner alone and without comfort or kindness. We came to save her, and there was no way I intended to leave without her. I bought a collar and a leash from the shelter volunteers, and Jack carried her out to the car.

When we were halfway across the parking lot, she wiggled out of Jack's arms and ran like a bolt of lightning toward a busy road. Just as she turned and hesitated for a moment, Jack dove to the ground to catch her again. That initial run became a harbinger of what was to come. Cinderella—whom we renamed Ruby—was a runner. She could escape through a hole a quarter of her body size, and she was the fastest runner I'd ever seen. I spent many anxious moments chasing Ruby, cajoling her, begging her to come back home to warmth and safety.

"She needs a middle name," I said to Jack as our new pup burrowed under a blanket in the corner, making herself as invisible as possible. "How about Ruby Rebecca?"

"Ruby Becky?" Jack asked. "That's kinda dumb. How about Ruby Doobie?"

"Like pot?" I asked.

Jack laughed. "Yeah, Mom. Like a doobie!"

"I can't name her Ruby Doobie," I said.

"Why not? It's perfect," Jack said. "And it rhymes. You like rhymes."

Eventually, the other kids talked me into Jack's suggestion, and Ruby Doobie was christened.

For the first couple of weeks in her new home, Ruby didn't want anything to do with us. She never made eye contact, didn't wag her tail, didn't bark. After thoroughly examining my fence for breaches, I'd open my back door to let her out into the yard, and she'd bolt from corner to corner, looking for a way out. Eventually, she'd run back in through my open door and curl up in a dark corner or under my couch.

Corners were her favorite. She'd make herself as small as possible, and she'd tuck her head into the crook of her own leg so she didn't have to see all the scary things that might come for her. I filled every corner of the house with blankets and pillows so she could find some comfort, but she didn't want comfort. She wanted to disappear.

When the kids and I sat watching TV at night, we let Ruby come to us. Every once in a while, she'd wander our way, sniffing and circling cautiously.

"Don't make eye contact," I'd whisper to the kids. "Pretend she's not here."

She was fascinated by Lucy's energy and uninterested in Maggie's lethargy. She would sprawl out on Lucy's big dog bed when Lucy wasn't around. She never stayed in one place for long.

I wanted to train Ruby, to control her, to teach her how to be social, to encourage her to sit on my lap and to walk on a leash by my side. But what Ruby wanted was to exist—carefully and deliberately—on her own terms. She sought out her corners of comfort, her little dens of quiet and darkness. If she visited me, I was grateful. If she didn't, I was still grateful. She was teaching me what she needed, and I was doing my best to listen.

One rainy Saturday morning, I sat on my screen porch with a book, a hot cup of coffee, and Lucy at my feet. I thought long and hard about how I might have lived and parented differently if I'd been brave enough to stand up for what I believed in.

There was a period of time when sweet Marley cried and begged to sleep in our bed at night. Charles would not hear of it.

"Let's just let her fall asleep with us, then we can move her back to her bed," I said.

"Absolutely not," he said. "This is not a community bed. This is our bed. And she needs to learn how to self-soothe." He was a stickler for the kind of parenting John Rosemond proposed in his *Six-Point Plan for Raising Happy, Healthy Children* book. My innate belief system ran more along the lines of free-range parenting with some established boundaries, but I had never been responsible for small children before I had my own. Charles, however, as the youngest of four by a number of years, had cared for many of his nieces and nephews, and I believed him to be more of an expert than I was. So, I eschewed my natural parenting instincts and supported him in his beliefs. As John Rosemond said, it was important for us to parent in agreement.

When Marley cried at night, I thought about the wolves that I was certain lived under my bed as a child, and all I wanted to do was keep them from my daughter. But Charles had convinced me that a family bed was not an option.

As a result, I would find my curly-haired toddler with the rosy cheeks on the floor outside my bedroom door most mornings. With her pink blankie in hand and her pointer and middle finger in her mouth, she'd cry herself to sleep in that spot night after night.

How hard would it have been to give her those little pockets of comfort when she needed us most? Why was I so weak that I wouldn't stand my ground? How many salty tears did that small patch of carpet soak up?

Withholding love, comfort, physical touch—it was against my nature. Every morning, when I scooped her small, sweaty body into my arms, I silently begged her forgiveness.

It was such a small ask. Such a reasonable one. Safety, comfort, security. And somehow, I'd been convinced to say no. We make a lot of concessions as parents—it's important, after all, to find a place of compromise when multiple people are involved. But when you sacrifice who you are at the core to be who someone else thinks you should be, it's entirely unsustainable. Like a promise made and broken over and over again.

CHAPTER 23

I slid gently into forty-seven with coffee and contemplation on the chilly front porch of my little white rented cottage. Lucy sat by my side, snoozing and sighing heavily in the morning air as I thought about my life thus far.

Birthdays have always been a time in which I find myself reflective, introspective, even a bit melancholy, but not necessarily in a sad way. I'm not concerned about aging, and I'm learning to love my life and myself a little more every day. I enjoy the wisdom and perspective that comes with age, the learning.

By forty-seven, I learned there are people who are beautiful on the outside and empty in the middle. That when you take a bite, expecting a solid, satisfying experience, they crumble in your hands like hollow milk chocolate. A fleeting pleasure, unsustainable.

I learned that some people will say words like *love* and *forever* and still leave you crying on the floor in a heap of confusion and pain.

I learned that those people include me.

I learned it's okay and necessary to say words like *no*, and *that's enough*, and *I'm done*, and *I'm sorry*. And I learned when someone says you've hurt them, they need you to know. To listen. To acknowledge.

I learned we all get to live our lives the best way we know how. We all get to love in whatever way works for us. That societal rules don't always fit everyone equally. That belief systems are personal and complex and sacred. That we get to define our lives and loves with honesty and careful consideration. That the shackles of *what should be* can be thrown off to welcome *what is* instead. That the beauty of life is in the choices we make—for our loved ones, our friends, our families, ourselves. That our hearts will guide us if we listen and let them.

I learned my sensitivity isn't a weakness, but my strength instead. Vulnerability, kindness, authenticity—those are my Super Powers. This is the cape I wear proudly. I don't want to be tough and hard-hearted. I want to cry. To feel it all. And that also doesn't mean I want to be mistreated. Or used. Or thrown away carelessly. Sensitivity, self-care, and self-respect can coexist. I'm learning how to make a home in my heart for all of them.

I learned that Sara Barielles' *Gravity* will always bring me to my knees.

And that love isn't about leaning, but about lifting. About walking together, side-by-side, about choosing that companionship every damn day. Even when it's hard. Especially when it's hard. That falling into someone else's gravity is a surrender. And that we should never, ever surrender ourselves to another. Because without our own core, we have nothing to offer—to ourselves, to anyone else. And so, it's also okay to let go when a relationship has run its course. Not just okay, but right. And necessary.

I learned that time is my love language. That face-to-face interactions fuel and fill me. That I desperately miss those whose distance keeps me from hugging and holding them. That I appreciate the ones who move heaven and earth to spend time with me. That the effort itself is the love. That I'm learning how to give it back—in whatever form is needed—on the other side. That all our lives are busy, but if we don't make time for what really matters, then nothing really matters.

And I learned that I don't matter to some. That I'm not a priority for those who cannot make time for me—no matter how much I want to be. That I cannot force someone to see me if she's unwilling to look. I'm learning to navigate that knowledge with grace and acceptance. Still learning. Always learning.

I learned that authenticity and introspection are vital to me. That I don't want to be a person who is blind to my own faults and shortcomings. That I don't want to invite those who are blind to their own faults and shortcomings into my life. The *always-rights*. The *my-way-or-the-highways*. The *the ways* versus the *a ways*. That I can kiss them and wish them well and that we'll both be better humans for having let go.

In the past year, I felt sand between my toes, heard the crash of the open waves, held starfish in my hands, flew through cumulus cotton candy clouds, traversed mountain roads and trails, explored bustling city streets, tasted new foods and exquisite wines, and came back home to rest fireside with dogs and kids and love and solid ground.

I sent my firstborn son to college, watched his life become more his and less mine.

I lost sixty-five pounds, two kidney stones, and a relationship I thought would be forever. And in that lesson, I lost my expectations of others and learned to love them (which sometimes includes letting them go) right where they are instead.

I was hurt by those I love most.

I hurt those I love most.

I went back on anti-depressants and anti-anxiety meds because sometimes the world is just too much, too big, too glorious, too bright, too challenging for me to walk through with any semblance of grace and balance. It's like wearing those gorgeous high-heeled pumps that make your calves look fabulous and turn your weak ankles at the same time. And I learned that it's okay to switch to your running shoes when necessary—for comfort and support and safety. Life is a balance. Yin/Yang.

I learned the suicide rate among middle-aged people is steadily increasing. That midlife is a turning point that drives many to choose an end over a new beginning. That I feel the pressure, the sadness of it sometimes. But that I also see the light and opportunity and adventures ahead. That I choose to run toward that instead—despite the obstacles that may thwart the journey.

I watched my mother's health decline, experienced the transformation of her house to accommodate the transformation of her failing body. Eventually stood by her nursing home bed and held her frail hands in that space where she never wanted to reside.

I stood with my daughter as she attended her sophomore Homecoming dance with her first girlfriend. We got to discuss what it means for her to be attracted to both male and female. We got to discuss what it has always meant for me as well. The biggest *me, too* of our lives, my girl and me. How far we've come societally, how far we've yet to go. How sacred and profound love is, how gentle and precious and often misunderstood.

I publicly revealed pieces of my past—sexual abuse, sexual assault—that both broke and made me. I got to bear witness to those whose stories were parallel. To hold space for them. They did the same. We broke for each other again and again. And then we held, lifted, carried on, created something beautiful from the pieces we discovered in the aftermath. Because as Ram Dass so beautifully states, "We're all just walking each other home."

I got to experience again—on the edge of a precipice—what true love and commitment is about. What forgiveness and grace resemble.

I learned that nothing stays the same. And that this reality will simultaneously make and break us. And that if we understand and embrace and welcome those changes, we get to grow and reinvent and rediscover what we love most about each other and about ourselves.

I learned that life is a great unraveling, and that I've only begun to scratch the surface.

I learned that I have so much yet to learn.

* * *

In my 40th year, seven years earlier, I ran my first and only marathon. A bucket list item, a personal challenge. A 26.2-mile run at a 15-minute per mile pace gives you lots of time to think. People have often asked, "What was the hardest part about running a marathon?"

And my answer is never simple or straightforward. "All of it. And none of it."

The biggest commitment was the training time, hours and hours alone on the back roads of Zanesville, Indiana, headphones blaring, thighs burning, cars honking, horses grazing on the roadsides. But the time alone was also the benefit, time to reflect, time to listen to my favorite 80s songs without my kids yelling, "Mom! You're killing us with that music!"

Nothing, for me, is really ever black and white; nothing is absolute. I live in the gray where questions are often unanswered and there is room for uncertainty, for a change in direction.

Running a marathon had always been a goal for me—an accomplishment to check off before I turned 40. True to my procrastinating nature, however, I began training at 39 and crossed the finish line when I was well on my way to 41. What I have learned, though, is this: it doesn't matter when we do something that needs to be done as long as we do it. Forty was an arbitrary age, 26.2 a random goal. The important thing was what happened in between—sixty pounds lost, strength and stamina and perspective gained.

The open road has many lessons to impart.

At mile eighteen of the 2010 Indianapolis Monumental Marathon, my then-husband and kids waited. Charles had Gu and Gatorade and words of encouragement.

"You're a rock star," he said, squirting fruit punch flavored electrolytes into my mouth. "Are you okay?"

"I'm great!" I said.

And I was. After eighteen miles, I was still running, albeit slowly.

"Can I run with you for a while?" Scott asked. It was his fourteenth birthday. We had plans to go out to dinner that night to celebrate. I looked at my teenager, still a child but peeking into the vast abyss of manhood. He and Jack, the baby at age nine, jogged beside me in front of the Indianapolis Art Museum. Austin and Marley stayed with their dad.

"Go, Mom, go!" Marley yelled as we ran by Robert Indiana's iconic LOVE sculpture. Soon, Scott and Jack fell away and rejoined Charles and the other kids. I soldiered on, slowly plodding, regaining a cadence that was steady and sure, adjusting my headphones, setting my sights on the ruby and orange leaves in the distance.

Running a marathon is a solo endeavor. Yes, there are runners beside you and in front of you and behind you. (For me, they were mostly in front, while the people behind me were the ones packing up the water stations.) My family and friends met me at certain mile markers with cameras and cheers and

Clif Shot Bloks. But the miles themselves were my own, the pacing decisions entirely up to me, the stamina internal.

Along the way, you may trip, you may pull muscles, you may head down the wrong street. During a late-night training run, I once became dehydrated and disoriented. I threw up on the side of the road, lay down in the grass, and called my family to gather and take me home.

That is the best we can ask for, isn't it? That at the end of our journey—no matter what missteps we might have made, or how quickly (or slowly) we might have crossed the finish line, or how many toenails we left in our wake, or how many others we might have unintentionally tripped along the way—there is someone. Someone kind and faithful and true, someone who believes in you when you've stopped believing in yourself, someone who holds the water bottle to your parched lips and says, "Good run, love. You made it. Well done."

And the best person for that job?

You.

Always you.

EPILOGUE

In the aftermath of the storm, there is a hot, reverent silence. There is an ominous humidity in the air; a heavy, reluctant apology. As the survivors sift through what remains—pictures, furniture, scattered clothes, lamps, curtains, the remnants of a once-happy home—there is a humid hush. A space where memories exist, where mourning roosts, where tomorrow seems as irrelevant as a thousand broken yesterdays.

Often, there are tears. Of loss, regret, sadness. They have to come, these inevitabilities. They are what make us human, after all. Who among us hasn't loved and lost? Who hasn't succumbed to the force of the winds, the blinding gale? Who hasn't walked into the darkness, face upturned, drenched by the torrential downpour, and said, *Take me. Here I am. Do with me what you will.*

Perhaps those of us who haven't really lived.

There are, of course, questions: *What just happened? What could we have done differently? What comes next?*

But in the moments immediately after, there is just the now. The roar of the hurricane might still ring in your ears, but there is a rainbow on the horizon. It is visible beyond the gray-blue clouds, and a light sprinkling of rain cools your heated skin. Your skin has always been too hot, too much.

The one who opened this door often said that about you.

You have always been too much.

But there are others who love those pieces of you, who appreciate that too much is who you are. It is your essence. And they embrace all of it.

Some of those people you know.

Some you have not yet met.

But you will find them.

There are so many you don't know yet who will end up loving you. A lifetime of love and opportunity. What a beautiful thought, what a reassurance.

You might never find the photo album from your wedding day in the wet, dirty debris. You may never locate the rocking horse that was stored for so many years in the attic or the artwork created by your precious babies' hands.

But your people?

They're there.

They're all that matters.

Rain-soaked and muddy and disheveled, they are looking for you, calling for you, finding you.

Look up from the wreckage.

See them.

Know them.

Embrace them.

After the storm, if they're still there sifting through what remains with you, they are meant to stay.

And you?

You are meant to stay, too.

Every beautiful, battered, bruised, authentic piece of you.

Enjoy more about
Hurricane Lessons

Meet the Author
Check out author appearances
Explore special features

ABOUT THE AUTHOR

KATRINA ANNE WILLIS'S debut novel, *Parting Gifts*, was published in 2016. Her work has been featured in *The New York Times*, *Huffington Post*, *YourTango*, and *Mamalode*, as well as in numerous anthologies with subjects ranging from female friendship to grief. She was named one of six distinguished authors at the 2016 Indianapolis Book & Author Luncheon, was a BlogHer Voice of the Year in 2015, and was a 2011 Midwest Writers Fellow. A mother of four amazing adults and two special needs rescue dogs, Katrina currently writes and resides in Lexington, Kentucky.

ACKNOWLEDGMENTS

The acknowledgments section, for me, is always the most daunting part of creating a book. Not because it's difficult to thank so many people, but because I have so many people to thank. An embarrassment of riches, you might say. I'm paralyzed by the fear of forgetting someone. That is the price to pay for a life of love and support and abundance, though, so I will gladly pay it.

First and foremost, I want to thank Julia Park Tracey who said yes. The publishing business is a brutal one, filled with far more rejections than acceptances. But it just takes one yes, and Julia said it exuberantly. This book would not exist in the world without you, my friend. And to the rest of the Sibylline Press team, especially Vicki DeArmon, Suzy Vitello, and Anna Termine: What an amazing publishing experience you have provided me. And this cover, Alicia Feltman! It still overwhelms me with its beauty.

To Alice Anderson, my brilliant, supportive developmental editor who saw *Hurricane Lessons* in its earliest form and knew exactly how to guide it into being. Your expert advice, your thoughtful notes, your presence in my life: I am so grateful for all of them, Alice.

To Suzette Mullen and the Write Yourself Out writers: My eternal gratitude for creating the safe space it took to write that excruciating query letter and proposal. And to Jenny Haliski who raised her hand as a beta reader and provided such meaningful feedback. It was wonderful sharing that sacred online space with you all.

To the ones who have supported me every step of the way with their words, their actions, their pocketbooks, and their enthusiasm. Rachel Macy Stafford, you have always been my guiding light in the world of words. Your friendship is balm to my often-weary soul. Amy Ferris, your indomitable spirit and your words of encouragement fuel me every single day. Debbie Dyson, Debra Davis, and Jodi Nixon, I'm not sure I could ever find more dedicated readers. Bri Nightingale, thank you so much for reading my early words and for your and Abby's treasured friendship. Matt Bays and Kate Mapother, you are my go-tos in both success and sadness. I know I can trust you with my tears, my happiness, my insecurities, and my joys. What gifts you are in my life.

Andrea Spiegelberg, Katy Allen, Heather Carson, and Kerri Suhr, what would I do without your solid, sustaining, lifelong friendship? You are truly the ones who have taken me on in sickness and in health, till death do us part. It is rare to find such lasting friendships. I count you among my greatest treasures.

To my cousins, my first and forever friends, and to my hilarious and loving aunts and uncles. Growing up in such a circle of happiness and joy was a gift I can never repay. Thank you all for a strong set of roots, songs around campfires, and so many magical memories. Being a part of this extended family is a gift beyond measure. And to my late stepdad, Bob, who was never really a *step*, but a *forever*. And to his kids and their families who became my family, too.

To Courtney Maum and Jeannine Ouellette, who irrevocably changed my writing with their wisdom, grace, generosity, and guidance.

To Libby Clark, the first to read and hold these words so carefully as we were making our way into each other's lives. Thank you for giving them—and me—such a soft place to land. Thank you for being the first to show me the beauty of a same-sex love and partnership. You will forever hold a piece of my heart in your hands.

I lost my beloved mom and my only sister while I was writing this book. There are days the resounding ache of those losses is the only thing I can feel. But then I remember instead how it felt to be held in the arms of such beautiful, loving women. Our little female power trio from the jump. Caroline Mary (Sis) Anderson Weaver and Carrie Ellen (Hodge) Smith, I know you're cheering me on—with Keoke coffees in hand—from the eternal stardust. Thank you, too, Carrie, for giving me Kevin, Amber Marie, and Anderson McGuire. And for loaning me your BFF, Jan, who makes the best snickerdoodles in the universe.

Sam, Augustus, Mary Claire, and George, no matter how many books I may write in my lifetime, you four will always be my greatest works. Thank you for choosing me as your mom, for giving me the experience of ushering you into this world. What remarkable humans you have all become.

And to Julie Gallutia, who has stood beside me through so much love and loss and celebration and mourning. To Julie who brings me coffee in the morning and wishes me sweet dreams every night. To Julie who co-parents our sweet pups, Ruby and Sissy, and overcooks my chicken just the way I like it. To Julie who takes care of my every need before I even know I need it. To Julie, my pickleball partner and dance partner and euchre partner. To Julie who makes every day magic.

As the incomparable Cheryl Strayed once said, "Be brave enough to break your own heart." I will forever be indebted to everyone who so graciously and generously helped heal this one.

STUDY GUIDE QUESTIONS:

1. How do organized religion and societal expectations play a role in Katrina's story?

2. How did you feel about Cecilia's overall treatment of Katrina? Why did Katrina choose to stay in the relationship as long as she did?

3. Do you believe Katrina fell into love, lust, limerence, or something else when she met Cecilia?

4. Do you think Charles was justified in having Katrina involuntarily committed? Was she a threat to herself or to others?

5. How do you think Katrina's actions impacted her children? Was it more important for her to maintain the family structure for the benefit of her kids or to show them the importance of being true to oneself?

6. What are your thoughts about Charles's and Jess's early relationship? Was Katrina justified in her anger and resentment when they had sex in their shared home?

7. What are your thoughts about Katrina and Charles's decision to open up their marriage to other lovers? Could this have been a viable solution to the dilemma they faced?

8. Were there issues that contributed to the demise of the marriage beyond Katrina's queer realization?

9. Do you think you would have been a friend who stayed (like Allison) or a friend who shunned (like Mia)?

10. How can we, as a society, best demonstrate allyship to the LGBTQ+ community?

Griftopia: A Novel

By Suzy Vitello

FICTION

394 Pages • Trade Paper • $21
ISBN: 9798897400164
Also available as an ebook and audiobook

Orphaned sisters Pearl and Scarlett Freischin, each reeling from scandal and loss, must find a way to survive as their fractured family teeters on the edge of ruin. Desperate and nearly destitute, they turn to a string of dubious online schemes, exposing the darkly comic underbelly of modern hustle culture.

Last Summer at Feather River: A Novel

By Karen Nelson

FICTION

304 Pages • Trade Paper • $20
ISBN: 9798897400188
Also available as an ebook and audiobook

Ten years after a tragic accident closed her family's beloved Camp Feather River, Brooke returns to care for her grandfather and confront the past she's long avoided. As buried secrets surface, she begins to suspect that the so-called accident was something far more sinister.

The Newcomers: The Chronicles of Touperdu, Book I

By Pam Troy

FANTASY

472 Pages • Trade Paper • $22

ISBN: 9798897400089

Also available as an ebook and audiobook

In 1880, two immigrant families—a Creole chef seeking peace and a matriarch of witches craving freedom—journey to the mysterious Isle of Touperdu, hoping for a fresh start. But as they soon discover, the island's promise of refuge may be an illusion, forcing them to confront what they're willing to sacrifice to belong.

Sibylline Press is proud to publish the brilliant work of women authors over 50. We are a woman-owned publishing company and, like our authors, represent women of a certain age.

www.ingramcontent.com/pod-product-compliance
Lightning Source LLC
Jackson TN
JSHW020720090326
98940JS00005B/1610

* 9 7 9 8 8 9 7 4 0 0 1 4 0 *